Th...

The People of God

A Royal Priesthood

ALWYN MARRIAGE

DARTON·LONGMAN + TODD

253

First published in 1995 by
Darton, Longman and Todd Ltd
1 Spencer Court
140–142 Wandsworth High Street
London SW18 4JJ

ISBN 0–232–51989–7   20029875

A catalogue record for this book is available
from the British Library

Bible quotations are taken from
the New Jerusalem Bible,
published and copyright © 1985 by
Darton, Longman and Todd Ltd
and Doubleday & Co Inc.

Phototypeset by Intype, London
Printed and bound in Great Britain
by Page Bros, Norwich

Dedicated to the memory of
my father George Sherratt (1908–1983)
and my friend Christopher Bryant (1905–1985).

Acknowledgements

This book could not have been completed without the peace, facilities and stimulation afforded by a Rockefeller scholarship. Many thanks to those who awarded me the scholarship, and to the other international scholars who shared my residency at Bellagio.

For other opportunities for concentrated writing, away from the pressures of work, I should like to thank the Community of the Sisters of the Church, and the Bridgers.

I am grateful to the many Christians whose lives and ministry have inspired me to write this book; and in particular I should like to thank Sr Annaliese, Peter Doble, Lewis Elton, Ian Fisher, Janet Hodgkinson, Sophia and Zoë Marriage and Alwyn Sherratt for various forms of help and encouragement.

Above all, my thanks go to Hugh for sharing in gestation and birth.

Contents

1

On being the Church

This book is about priesthood: but it is not primarily concerned with ordination or the clergy. It is about ordinary
Christian people who live and work in the world, who
struggle with faith and doubt, who sin and are forgiven,
who try to follow Jesus Christ. The place of ordination within
the wider body of the Church will be considered: but the
emphasis is on the whole people of God, because it is all
Christians who are called to be part of a royal priesthood.

Many Christians do not realise that they are called to be
priests. The purpose of this book is to encourage the Church
to take Christian priesthood seriously: both the priesthood
of all believers and, within that, the ordained ministry. To
do this we shall look at the history, theory and practice of
the priesthood as we know it, and ask how closely these
accord with the Gospel and how effective they are in the
Church's mission to the world.

The ancient word, 'priest' is not altogether appropriate
for describing the ordained ministry of the Christian
Church, and many denominations have rejected it for that
reason. However, it is still probably the most widely understood term for ecclesiastical office holders, is current in the
largest world churches, and provides the model on which
many of the other, reformed, traditions have built their ministries. In what follows, therefore, when the word 'priest' is
used to describe those who are ordained, it refers equally to
all denominations.

Similarly, the word 'Church' should be understood to
refer to one, holy, catholic and apostolic Church to which
all the different denominations belong; and references to the

people of God, whether they be ordained or lay, cover
the varying traditions, regardless of the different titles that
are used to denote their clergy.

The churches' debate on priesthood

The controversies and disagreements of the Church over the
eligibility of certain groups of people to be ordained has
ensured that the term 'priest' has had its fair share of media
attention in recent years. This, however, has only served to
allow Christians to avoid the central issue of what priesthood
actually is. Although many people hold strong views on who
may or may not be ordained, the Church in general is
remarkably reticent about exploring the nature of priesthood
itself. It is hoped that the following pages may challenge
people to think about the nature of priesthood itself, and
begin to draw out what relevance that has to the lives of
ordinary women and men in the Church today.

November 11th 1992 marked a turning point in the history of the Church of England, as the day on which General
Synod finally approved the ordination of women within the
Anglican Church in England. For once, church debate made
headline news and words like 'priest', 'vocation' and 'ordination' were bandied around in the pub and on the commuter train as well as in the conference hall. The ripples
that spread out to so many of the other churches that day
were of excitement or of horror, depending on the differing
attitudes those churches had towards women's ordination.

Although the decision was greeted with varying shades of
relief or jubilation by the majority of Anglicans, there followed months of unedifying behaviour on the part of some
who were opposed to the change, and a number of people
claimed that it was the end of the road as far as ecumenism
with Rome was concerned. However, within weeks the cam-
paign for women's ordination was gathering momentum
amongst Roman Catholics and, despite opposition by the
Vatican, many consider that it is now only a matter of time
before the Roman Catholic Church capitulates over women

priests. Some Anglican clergy left their Church but by and large it would probably be true to say that the Church of England soon began to benefit from the influx of women priests more than it suffered from the departure of the disaffected.

Momentous as the historic vote appeared, and it is true that for a short time the debate and division attracted almost as much coverage in the national as in the religious media, the relief of many in the Church was not so much because a number of well-qualified women could now exercise their priesthood to the full, but because the Church of England was at last in a position to put the vexed question of women's ordination behind and turn attention to some of the vital aspects of the theology of priesthood that have received scant attention in recent years. The importance of opening the ordained priesthood to women should not be underestimated and the change will no doubt have repercussions in terms of our understanding of ordination; but after years of wrangling, it was high time that we left behind discussion of the gender of priests and began to look at the nature of priesthood itself.

No sooner had the Church of England licked its wounds from the battle over women's ordination, however, than a new controversy blew up and debate began to rage over whether or not it is acceptable for practising homosexuals to be ordained. When this has been resolved, will another excuse be found to avoid the central question? In the following chapters I shall attempt to unravel what priesthood meant in the Old and New Testaments, how it developed into its present forms, and what might be possible as we look to the future. The focus of this book, therefore, is on what priesthood is, rather than on who may or may not be ordained.

The clergy-lay barrier

Throughout Church history the respective roles of clergy and laity have occasioned dispute and controversy and the various attempts to limit papal, episcopal and clerical powers, by giving a degree of freedom and authority to the laity, have frequently led to discord and schism. One of the facts that was obscured by the debate over women's ordination was that lay *men* have not, in general, fared much better in the Church than women. As we examine the position of lay people of both sexes within the Church it would be as well to recognise that what has sometimes been paraded as male chauvinism might, in fact, be interpreted as nothing more nor less than a wholesale and long-standing devaluation of the laity by the clergy.

Conversely, lay people in the Church who, for one reason or another, have had a negative experience of clergy, sometimes develop a cynicism about priesthood as a whole. The anti-clericalism that recurs fairly frequently in church history is a result of an unhelpful 'us and them' mentality, which is as much the fault of the laity as of the clerisy. If all Christians could put the ordained ministry into its true perspective, and begin to take responsibility for what the Church is and does, then this rift might be healed, and the Church cease to be perceived as a top-heavy power structure.

Belonging to a world-wide worshipping community should, and can, enable and strengthen people in the Christian faith. Far too many Christians, however, experience more pain and disillusionment in their dealings with the Church than they do in struggling to understand and live out their faith in the world.

Lay Christians are not the only ones who suffer from the artificial distinction between clergy and laity. Over the years many clergy have lived their lives sacrificially, only to find when they have spent their last ounce of energy in ministering to others, that it is difficult for them to seek or receive help from anyone who could offer adequate strength and support to them. They, just as much as the laity, can be the losers in a system that substitutes clericalism for a clear and consistent doctrine of Christian priesthood. However, above and beyond the damage done to Christian clergy and laity is the distortion of the identity of the Church that prevents the majority of people outside that institution from hearing and accepting the Gospel that is meant to bring life, not orthodoxy.

Crisis in the Church

Throughout history the Church has made mistakes, just like any other human institution. There has, for instance, been a tendency to control its members rather than freeing them: arousing guilt in people in order to then tell them that they are forgiven; preventing Christians from partaking of the sacraments, even though these would lead them into the presence of God; creating golden calves and demanding reverence; letting the naked emperor lead the procession and throwing anyone out if they giggled.

Lone voices have frequently been raised in protest; but as the second millennium draws to a close, a more fundamental and deep-seated dismay is afflicting the Church. 'Crisis in the Church' may smack a little of a juicy newspaper headline, but it would be difficult to deny that the Christian Church is suffering some form of crisis. There is room for discussion over what were the major causes of crisis, how long the present troubles have been brewing and what, if anything, can be done to save the Church as we have known it; but no one who cares deeply about the Church would pretend that all is well in Christendom. The more we love the Church and long to support and strengthen its mission in the world, the more imperative it is that we are honest about the present situation and try to face up to some of the questions that it raises.

For some the crisis stems from the increasing polarisation of Liberal, Catholic and Evangelical traditions. For others the feminist issue, either as it was manifested in the debate over the ordination of women, or in the more fundamental changes that feminist theology threatens to make to the structures of our faith, have rocked the boat almost to capsizing point. We hear exciting stories of the phenomenal growth of the Church in Africa and parts of South America, yet in much of the developed world there appears to be a constant drift away from the churches.

The Roman Catholic Church is discredited in Italy; the Anglican Church is reeling from financial problems in Britain; American Evangelical churches are rocked with scandals of greed and manipulation. In countries such as India the Church is mistrusted as a form of Western imperialism; in Western Europe it is ignored as irrelevant except for the occasional burst of scandal when a bishop re-interprets long-established doctrines or engages in irregular sexual practices.

Alongside these different crisis points, and contributing to them all in one way or another, is the crisis in the ordained ministry which is afflicting nearly all the mainstream Western churches. From the point of view of the clergy themselves this can be seen most dramatically in the drop in vocations, the increasing incidence of marital breakdown amongst clergy and the high levels of psychological distress and burnout commonly manifested either in minor outbreaks of depression and paranoia, or in more extreme cases of mental breakdown. There is a general unease amongst the clergy that all is not well, though few could put their finger on exactly what has gone wrong. We shall look later at some of the factors that contribute to this general loss of confidence, particularly the feelings of inadequacy and isolation that are bound to follow from the lack of a clear sense of identity.

From the point of view of the laity the crisis takes the form of widespread (though by no means universal) disillusionment with the clergy, exasperation with ecclesiastical hierarchies and a growing awareness that a Church that so consistently disables its adherents will never have the cutting edge when it comes to those divinely ordained commissions of mission and evangelism. Not only does the disablement of the laity frustrate many deeply committed Christians and limit the effectiveness of the Church in the world, but the very distinction between clergy and laity is itself unscriptural. The Greek word *laos* that we find in the New Testament means the whole people of God, and that includes everyone in the Church, regardless of whether they are ordained or not.

The deep-seated misunderstanding of the nature of the Church, that identifies Christianity with the clergy and defines the laity negatively as those who are not ordained, is not just an internal problem; for it has given a false idea of the Church to the world and prevented many people from finding their way to faith and salvation. We may regret that people confuse messenger with message; but the fact remains that the institution of the Church, in its various guises and forms, can be one of the major stumbling blocks people encounter in their search for a spiritual reality in their lives; and that the image many of these people have of the Church is deeply coloured by what the clergy say and do and are.

This came home to me forcibly in Russia recently, when a good, loving and generous woman was explaining to me why she is not a Christian. She told me that she respects what she has read of Jesus Christ, prays to God in the privacy of her own pillow, but cannot feel herself drawn to become part of a Church which she identifies with the unedifying squabbles of clergy over who should have possession of various churches and icons.

Variations on this theme recur all around the world, and it is unlikely that these are empty excuses for staying in bed on Sunday. Millions of people who express an urgent hunger for a spiritual dimension to their lives never get beyond a personal folk religion; others flirt with new religious movements, or battle on in isolation drawing what strength they can from art, or music or nature, because they do not feel that the Church will value them or the ideals that stir in their hearts.

Anyone who has worked in or for the Church will recognise that, in many social situations, to identify with that institution can be an immediate conversation-stopper. Most non-church-goers express some embarrassment at being caught anywhere near established religion; yet these same people, as soon as they are confident that no one is out to manipulate or convert them, frequently exhibit a fascination with the deep spiritual issues of life and are only too willing to discuss fundamental questions of faith.

This should come as no surprise, since the Church does not have a monopoly of spirituality; but what is almost unbearably frustrating for any Christian who tries to live out their love for God and humanity in the world, is the yawning gap between the irrelevance into which Christianity is so often pushed, and the desperate and largely unsatisfied need that people have to receive the Gospel. Where are we going wrong?

The stirring of hope

Plato, in the *Meno*, demonstrates how learning can begin only at the point where we become aware of our own bafflement and lack of understanding. For anyone who has been involved in teaching, this is clearly true, and the student or child who thinks she knows it all is unlikely to make much progress in education. The Church, which entered recent history as an influential institution well used to holding the reins of power, education, culture and wealth had such an unshakable faith in its own superiority that there was little room for growth or learning. It may well be that the very crises that threaten to make life uncomfortable for the Church in the coming decade offer the possibility of salvation, and that from the embers of our arrogant superiority might rise the phoenix that will bring new life not just to us but to the whole world.

For crisis is not necessarily a bad thing. It takes the carpet away from under our complacency and nudges us towards a reassessment and redirection of our vocation. Much has been made of the fact that the Chinese word for 'crisis' is made up of two symbols, one of which means 'danger' and the other 'opportunity'. The experience of many people who have faced up to some kind of crisis in their own lives is that this can be a time of unparalleled development and the tilling of a richer soil in which the seeds of deeper joy can grow.

A Church that offers cosy options, that is a haven for

those who fear change or whose complacent belief that they are right cuts them off from other people, has little in common with the subversive ministry of Jesus Christ, who overturned not just the tables of the money lenders, but the preconceived ideas of an upright moral society and the sacred assumptions of the religious establishment of his day. The very fact that the Church now engages in the turmoil of modern life and thought and morality is a sign of hope for the future; and the wounds that will be sustained might well bring a closer identification with the reality of love shown in Christ crucified.

One area in which crisis might lead to growth is in the matter of vocations to the ordained ministry; for, as fewer educated and committed Christians feel drawn to ordination, the more well-informed Christians there may be out in the world, evangelising, loving and living the Gospel of Christ. If this is so, then we should at least consider the possibility that the drop in vocations in itself might be one manifestation of the work and guiding of the Holy Spirit in the Church today.

It is arguable that the very last thing we should do to bright and committed young Christians is to separate them from the world in which they are living out the Gospel; yet there is still an assumption abroad that the principal and preferred way to express a deep commitment to Christ is to 'go into the Church'. This phrase in itself shows the extent of our misunderstanding, for surely the very least that can be said of *any* Christian is that she or he has 'gone into the Church'?

The fact that many deeply committed Christians are now prepared to live out their Christian vocation without the protection of special title, or identifying garments, or the power of an institution behind them if they get it wrong, bodes well for the Church in the coming years. Many of the most worthwhile secular charities are staffed predominantly by Christians, who find such work a more viable way of living out their faith than adopting positions within the Church.

If the Christian Church is inspiring people, particularly perhaps young people, with the Gospel so that they can work for the poor and needy, it cannot be said to be lacking in vocations. Only when this is recognised will we start to invest wholeheartedly in training the laity to fulfil that vital ministry and to make sense of the biblical concept of the priesthood of all believers.

Rediscovery of the laity

In recent years several of the major churches have begun to explore the hypothesis that the future of the Church might lie in developing a viable and responsible laity, through training programmes and some sharing of the decision-making process and pastoral work of the Church.

Increasingly over the last few decades there has been a call for a clearer appreciation of the part lay people have to play in the Church, partly as a result of the deliberations of the Roman Catholic Church at the Second Vatican Council in the early 1960s.[1] Since then councils and synods have continued to explore the reality of lay catholicism and how this might affect the future of the Church in terms of both leadership and identity; and the post-Vatican II years have brought the gradual realisation to many Roman Catholics that the future of the Church lies in the laity.

Despite this formal revelation, however, odd assumptions, inherited from two thousand years of history, die hard. These assumptions, that the Church ultimately is the clergy and that the height of Christian vocation is to become a priest, are still firmly etched into the consciousness of the Roman Catholic Church as an immutable distinction between what the Council called the 'common priesthood of the faithful' and the hierarchical priesthood: 'The ministerial priest, by the sacred power he enjoys, moulds and rules the priestly people.'[2]

The same distinction between ordained and lay people has traditionally characterised the Anglican Church; and the cynical definition of the position of the laity as 'on its knees with its hands in its pockets' is not as far-fetched and amusing as one might think. However, the Church of England, too, began to be aware of the lay people who fill, or fail to fill, its pews; and in 1985 the General Synod commissioned a report entitled *All are called; Towards a theology of the Laity.* This report, if a little thinner on theology than the ruminations of the Vatican dignitaries, was a more eminently readable document which not only contributed a positive statement of lay Christianity to the debate, but also made a number of practical suggestions for positive action rather than remaining at the level of theory.

The Free Churches are often assumed to have inherited from the Reformation a system that is less hierarchical. However, despite many excellent initiatives in the training and utilisation of the laity, the free churches are in general just as clergy-dominated as the older traditions. In fact, in a Church where the central action is the preaching of the word rather than the celebration of the sacraments, the officiant can take on something approaching a celebrity role, with the result that the merits of a service are often judged primarily by how good the preacher is. The very position and height of the pulpit in some Nonconformist churches is in itself indicative of the exaggerated importance of the minister in those communities.

Like Roman Catholics and Anglicans, many Nonconformists are now examining the position of lay people within the Church, and recognising that wisdom and expertise do not necessarily, or uniquely, descend at the moment of ordination or grow to maturity thereafter.

Various documents have been produced in the different churches in response to these developments and the subject has been widely debated at conferences and synods. A number of questions remain unresolved, including the extent to which lay people are to exercise their ministry in the Church of the future, and how they are to be trained and authorised for leadership. But no discussion that treats lay ministry in isolation from the doctrine of Christian priesthood will advance the theology or practice of the Church. For ultimately, to define the laity as those who are not priests will undermine not only the effectiveness of the people of

God in the world, but also the ministry that is offered by ordained women and men.

At the same time as the different denominations have been waking up to the fact that there is rather more to the Church than the ordained ministry, scholars have been studying the history and theology of priesthood and concluding that Christian priesthood as we know it was not instituted by Christ and in fact did not emerge in the Church until at least the end of the second century (see chapter 5). However, despite this new emphasis on the laity on the one hand, and the putting of ordained ministry into more honest perspective on the other, there has been little attempt to explore how these factors should be influencing the way in which the Church operates in the future.

But perhaps the greatest cause for hope lies in the organic growth of lay Christianity in recent years. Whether it be in a poor base community in Latin America, where lay people have taken the initiative because there is no trustworthy priest for miles around; or a community of lay people who are trying to live together in rural Britain according to the model of the early Church; or a housegroup that meets once a week, or once a month, to argue and pray, worship and support each other: the people of God have been beginning to take responsibility for their own spiritual formation and education. They do not need to seek permission, or leadership, or authentication from an ordained priesthood; for what they are discovering as they share their lives and experiences, is that they are the people of God.

The concept of *koinonia*, to which the World Council of Churches has drawn attention in recent years, has no exact equivalent in English, but something of its flavour is suggested by words like 'community', 'communion', 'sharing', 'fellowship', 'participation' and 'solidarity'. What the pilgrims to the World Council of Churches Faith and Order Conference in Santiago de Compostela in 1993 discovered was that all over the world Christians from churches of different traditions are exploring their common life in Christ, and learning that commitment to Christ does not mean going to church so much as 'being Church'.

Towards a vision of one Church

Much of the loss of direction clergy have experienced this century, as well as lay people's distrust of the clergy, could be attributable to a lack of vision, and to confusion over the true nature of priesthood. 'Where there is no vision the people perish' (Prov. 29:18) sang one of the poets of the Old Testament. If we fail to nurture a vision of priesthood in our own times, we should not be surprised to find that priesthood is perishing.

The Christian Church did not spring into existence with a ready-made doctrine of priesthood, but has had to beaver away at it over the centuries, adapting and developing in response to changing circumstances. We have as much responsibility to that ongoing process and development as the Christians of any former age.

Discussion of the Church, the whole people of God, must include an analysis of what priesthood is; and conversely, discussion of Christian priesthood is going to make sense only within the wider context of the Church. For priest and people are involved in the same endeavour. They share a calling, a commitment and a mission to the world. As long as a wedge is driven between priest and people, all Christians will suffer the pain of being a divided Church.

There is nothing particularly radical in recognising that the Church has become too clericalised, that the future of Christianity depends to a great extent on the empowering of the laity, or even that all Christians are called to share in priesthood. Indeed, much the same questions, criticisms and recommendations have recurred throughout the history of Christianity with surprising regularity. But for some reason these truths do not appear to have filtered through into changed consciousness and action. They should not just be interesting academic debating points, but the material out of which we forge a clearer vision that will enable the Church to live out her true vocation in the world.

Karl Marx, in concluding his Communist Manifesto, claimed that the workers of the world had nothing to lose but their chains. Alan Webster, when he was Dean of St

Paul's Cathedral, once shared with me his adaptation of this into the clarion call for the empowerment of lay people: 'Laity of the world unite: you have nothing to lose but your clergy.' The solutions to the Church's problems may not lie in disbanding the institution of ordination; but if the creation of a Church that can speak to and for the people of God threatens the particular institutions that we have created and cherished over the years, then perhaps that is a risk we should be prepared to take.

There is no shortage of questions to be addressed; and although some may find these uncomfortable or even threatening, it should at least be acknowledged that they are real questions that it is legitimate for Christians to ask. How, for example, have we arrived at the state of affairs that now obtains? How was it that Christians, who were called to be free, succumbed to yet another form of subjugation as clergy power increased? What can be done about the abdication of responsibility for the Church displayed in the attitude of many of the laity? What is the priesthood for, and do we still need it today? What happens to the clergy if we do not? But along with all these other questions is the most important one, which is: how can all Christian people be enabled to enter into full and equal membership of the Body of Christ?

It would hardly be astonishing if some clergy resisted a re-analysis of the doctrine of priesthood. Any study that takes a fresh look at the advantages and disadvantages of ordination will worry those who feel threatened by the possibility of a conclusion that is critical of the present system. What if the ordained ministry were found to be an insupportable drag on the Church's dwindling resources? Would salaries and homes continue to be supplied to those who for many years have sacrificed advancement in other professions in order to serve the Church? Some will take an examination of the doctrine of priesthood as a personal criticism of their ministry; others as an ungodly attack on the time-honoured traditions of the Church. Whatever reassurances are offered, there will be some clergy who fear that their livelihoods, indeed their whole *raison d'être*, will be destroyed.

But the clergy are not the only ones with a vested interest

in maintaining the *status quo*, and if the ideas explored in this book contain any truth or justice, then the conclusions should be just as challenging to the laity. As has been found by those churches that have led the way in developing the participation of the laity, those who have not chosen to enter the ordained ministry sometimes take a deal of convincing that they are the Church. It is all very well to stand outside the tomb and call for Lazarus to come forth. The miracle of his emergence only makes any sense if Lazarus is happy to return to life.

All are called

One of the radical changes in religious consciousness that succeeded the life, death and resurrection of Jesus Christ was that divisions such as that between priest and people were superceded; and in the new order, all the faithful were equally called to relationship with God and had to accept full responsibility for the life and mission of the Christian community. Priesthood was no longer the preserve of the few, but the calling of all.

The flaw in most theological writings about priesthood is that they start by looking at the role of the ordained priest as something that can be clearly differentiated from that of the lay Christian. We shall see that this is unbiblical; for Christian priesthood, which in the New Testament means the priesthood exercised by all baptised Christians, is not something that sets one apart from other Christians, but something that defines one's membership of the larger Christian body. We belong to the Christian Church by virtue of the fact that we are members of a royal priesthood.

It is essential that the Church should now develop a whole-hearted and consistent vision of what it is to be a Christian, before looking at what might be the unique or special work of the ordained within the larger lay Church. In other words, by looking for a vision of priesthood independently of lay Christianity we have actually put the cart before the horse;

and getting the poor beast into harness and back on the road is not going to be a simple process.

So the vision we should seek is first and foremost a vision of the laity; then within that we might discover a vision of ordination that will build up the Church rather than diminishing it, and that will work effectively towards the evangelisation of a world which has little interest in the niceties of cultic office.

However, having accepted intellectually that not only have lay people been undervalued and clergy imbued with too much importance, but that the whole edifice of the clergy/lay distinction is founded on a mistaken understanding of the people of God, it is all too easy to treat the theorising as an end in itself while leaving the Church unchanged, in the forlorn hope that the problems will go away. Hand in hand with the forging of vision, therefore, must go an awareness that, vital though this is, it is not enough *just* to have vision. That vision must issue in practical action.

Enabling priesthood

Disabling is written into the very structures of the Church. This is perhaps best illustrated in the case of the Eucharist where, with shaky sacramental theology we have narrowed down the class of those who can make real the Eucharistic presence. Not only does this disempower the vast majority of Christians present at holy communion; it also means that the Church has been quite content, in places where there is no ordained priest, to deprive Christians of the most basic and life-sustaining sacrament, which many would consider vital to their souls' health. At the very least this deprivation must be questioned.

Having evolved a vision of priesthood within the wider Christian community, therefore, the practical issue that this book hopes to address is how the Christian Church can develop a priesthood that *enables* rather than *disables*. The gigantic leap from a clergy-centred Church to a people-centred Church should only be risked if it is clear that the

Holy Spirit is leading us into new truth and will guide and inspire us as we venture into the unknown. For what might emerge at the end of such a re-orientation may not bear a very close resemblance to the institution we have hitherto known.

Inspiring and guiding are two of the properties we most associate with the Holy Spirit. There is a two-fold purpose to this book: first to encourage the Church to develop a new *vision*; and second to try to discover ways in which that vision might be translated into *practical action*. It is therefore appropriate to invoke the Holy Spirit to inspire us in the forging of our vision and to guide us as we take our first tentative steps towards action.

We are a living Church: dynamic, developing, fallible, exciting. This book is offered to the Church as a celebration of the priesthood of all believers. It is an invitation to all Christians to exercise their baptismal priesthood, and is a challenge and encouragement to the ordained to consider how their priesthood can most effectively be exercised. For whether we have found our place in the baptised priesthood or the ordained priesthood, we share a common purpose and have a part to play in creating the Church of the future. We are the people of God.

2

Chosenness and covenant

The Bible contains the writings of many individuals and groups, from vastly different backgrounds and over thousands of years. It would be surprising, indeed, if there were uniformity in the materials that have come down to us; and in considering the documents we should always bear in mind the variety of traditions that are represented in the different writings.

It is not difficult to see this in the case of the Old Testament, where the styles, language and belief structures of the various sources can be clearly distinguished. It is also true, however, of the New Testament. The different gospel writers, for instance, reflect the traditions and concerns of their respective communities; and the epistles reveal to us the evolving theology of the early Church, in which congregations developed in a variety of ways, and in which a handful of creative thinkers and writers were gradually carving out a consistent theology.

There is limited value in appealing to the New Testament for a picture of what Christian priesthood is meant to be. For it is an inconvenient fact of history that not only do the gospels record no mention of such an institution by Jesus Christ, but even later, in the writings of and about the early Church, the word 'priest' is never used to refer to the leaders and teachers of the early Christian communities. However, as the early Church began to forge the beginnings of a recognisably Christian theology, various concepts from the Jewish Scriptures were taken up and developed in new and exciting ways.

In this chapter we shall examine two closely connected

concepts that lie at the root of Jewish religious consciousness and grow out of the early Israelites' attempts to explain the nature of their relationship with God. The first is the deep and fundamental faith of the Jewish people that they are God's chosen people; and following on from this is their understanding of the world as based on responsible relationship with God through the covenant. Having established the connection between these two foundation stones of being chosen and being called into covenant relationship with God, I shall proceed, in chapter 3, to trace the development of the concept of priesthood in the Old Testament, in order to understand why it was not seen as an appropriate model on which to build the idea of Christian leadership.

To treat the Old Testament writings as historical documents would be to grossly underestimate them and rob them of their power to influence the understanding and behaviour of humanity throughout history. A more fruitful approach is generally to regard them as a rich source of important and formative religious myths, and use them as the basis for a series of reflections on key concepts in Jewish and Christian thought.

Deep within Jewish religious consciousness is the belief that they were, in some strange and special sense, chosen by God. This concept, which I shall call 'chosenness', is one of the key concepts of the Old Testament; and it lies behind both our rationale for the present system of ordination and also the New Testament doctrine of the priesthood of all believers. For this reason it is also an appropriate place to start in our attempt to identify the roots of Christian priesthood.

Chosenness

A child, adopted in infancy, was suffering the normal traumas of adolescence and feeling sorry for himself for starting life at a 'disadvantage' until his mother pointed out that while most parents had to make the best of what came along when their children were born, he alone had actually been chosen.

We all long to be chosen. From the first honour bestowed on us by the child in the playground who wants to be our 'best friend', through the vagaries, delights and agonies of adolescent and adult relationships, to the astonished pride when we are offered a job that we thought would go to someone more deserving, or find fulfilment in the sacrament of marriage in which our choosing and our chosenness are merged, we derive incalculable pleasure from being the object of choice rather than necessity or duty. The contemporary poet, Tony Harrison, in his poem 'v', puts his finger not only on the sweetness but also the strength of choice in friendship:

> The ones we choose to love become our anchor
> when the hawser of the blood-tie's hacked, or frays.[1]

Throughout the Scriptures we read of individuals being 'chosen' by God to be or do something special. Jacob, David, Solomon, Jeremiah and many others were conscious of being chosen by God for a specific task; and the same concept spills over into Christian thought in the title for Jesus Christ of 'the chosen one of Israel'. But in the Old Testament it was not just these leaders of the community who had the honour of being chosen, for the early Jewish people came to believe that their race was, in some peculiar sense, 'chosen' by God. This confidence that they were 'chosen' by God as a special nation became a vital part of Jewish identity at an early date and has marked their history for better and worse even since.

This is obviously a dangerous claim to make, and not one that is likely to endear any nation to those outside its charmed circle. Favourite children soon become unpopular and find themselves excluded from the games of their peers; and similarly, claims to be a unique and special people can unfortunately end up with the wearing of yellow stars. A wrong understanding of the Jewish assurance of being a 'chosen race' would soon degenerate into racism; and the Jews, who have suffered from this scourge more than most peoples, should be the first to avoid the pitfalls of such a misunderstanding. What the early Jewish people came to understand was that to be chosen by God is to be called into relationship with the divine. The Old Testament writings therefore make it clear that being chosen brought with it an imperative that these people should serve and obey their God.

Uncomfortable, and open to misinterpretation as it is, gentiles cannot politely ignore the Jewish claim to be God's chosen race. Rather they must confront it and engage with it, for this concept of 'chosenness' which grew in the hearts of early Jewish people as they explored their relationship with God contains the kernel of one of the most important truths that have dawned on the religious sensibility of humankind: namely that humanity is chosen and precious to God, that God cares deeply and personally for each and every person in the world. Within the context of the tribal and territorial conflicts of the ancient Near East, the concept was bound to be particularised; but the truth behind it, which so many of the other primitive peoples failed to grasp, is that humanity is part of the loving design of a beneficent and personal God.

This kernel was, of course, overlaid with other aspects of a primitive society's understanding of divinity and coloured by lonely attempts to make sense of their awareness of and respect for divinity in the midst of alien and pagan cultures. Because of this there is no doubt that the early Jews *did* particularise their revelation that God had chosen them; and they certainly did not see this in the terms I have suggested, as being a symbol for all humanity in relation to God. So we read in Deuteronomy the text on which the Petrine passage concerning the priesthood of all believers is based: 'For you are a people consecrated to Yahweh your God; of all the peoples on earth, you have been chosen by Yahweh your God to be his own people' (Deut. 7:6).

However, with the benefit of the revelation of God made available through the incarnation of Jesus Christ, the Jewish claim to be a chosen race can be understood as a vivid life-giving symbol of the truth that humanity is chosen and loved by God. The point is not that they, or we, are chosen in contra-distinction to others, but that they and we can show others what it means to be chosen.

All are chosen

The human race is special to God, for we are made in the image of God and have borne within our humanity the divine being in the person of Jesus Christ. Humanity has shown itself peculiarly resistant to accepting the truth that all we have and are is created by God, through the love of God, for the love of God. The concept of being chosen helps to give assurance that life is not arbitrary and senseless, but alive with divine meaning. So the Jewish race, as we read in the Old Testament stumbled its way from the dawn of history, typical of any other group of people, with the whole gamut of character defects and mistakes that characterise humanity. They were not especially good, or clever, or sensitive, but they understood intuitively that they were loved in all their humanity by God, the source of all.

It is fundamental to our faith that God chooses humanity, creating the world to be in loving creative relationship with the divine nature. The Jews saw this before others, even if they particularised it too much; and for that reason they tried to live out an intense and intimate relationship with God.

> Yahweh set his heart on you and chose you, not because you were the most numerous of all peoples – for indeed you were the smallest of all – but because he loved you and meant to keep the oath which he swore to your ancestors. (Deut. 7:7, 8)

Over the centuries, the Jews passed on anecdotes that showed what it was to recognise one's chosenness. By relating stories, celebrating our sacred history, we, too, can come to recognise our value and the *raison d'être* for our lives.

Because Jesus was a Jew, and Christianity evolved out of the Jewish religion, it has been tempting for the Church to adopt the attitude that Christians are God's new chosen people. This is not only insulting to Jews, suggesting that God has now abandoned them and chosen new favourites; but also completely misses the point that the concept of 'chosenness' makes available to us. The Christian Church, breaking out of the racial straitjacket that constrained the Jews, had – and has – the opportunity to take this important revelation of the Jews and pass it on to the world. 'Chosenness' in a wrong sense will lead the Church into pride and intolerance; but understood in a more symbolic and flexible way it is a catalyst for mission. Jesus Christ, as the Son of God who was born to identify with ordinary people, further substantiates this truth, that humanity is chosen and special to God.

The constancy of God

In Deuteronomy 30 we read of another revelation that came to this perceptive, theistic people:

> Had you wandered to the ends of the heavens, Yahweh your God would gather you even from there, would come there to reclaim you and bring you back to the land your fathers possessed, so that you in your turn might make it your own, prospering there and increasing even more than your fathers. (vv. 4–5)

This trust, that however far we wander from God, when we turn back we will be welcomed, was later to be picked up by Jesus Christ in the parables he told. For Jesus it was essential to an understanding of the nature of God: but fresh as it is when it re-emerges in the early years of the first century AD, its essence is already here, deep in the psyche of the Jewish nation, that God is faithful and forgiving.

In a primitive society, surrounded by unfriendly nations and at the mercy of plague, drought and ignorance, belief in a constant God brought dignity, responsibility and hope to this developing nation. Isaiah was later to comfort the people

by reminding them of the continuing friendship that God
had chosen to bestow on their nation:

> But you, Israel, my servant, Jacob whom I have chosen,
> descendant of Abraham my friend, whom I have taken to
> myself, from the remotest parts of the earth and sum-
> moned from countries far away, to whom I have said, 'You
> are my servant, I have chosen you, I have not rejected
> you', do not be afraid, for I am with you; do not be
> alarmed, for I am your God. (41:8–10)

As they grappled with the nature of God, the Jews were
also thrashing out what became a highly sophisticated moral
code. It was clear to them that some ways of living are
substantially better than others, and that these would naturally be more favoured by God. This they expressed in
terms of striking a bargain, or covenant, with God and then
keeping their human side of this covenant. But this relationship and the ethical code to which it gave rise were only
possible because first and foremost God had loved and
chosen them.

It is not too far-fetched to interpret this attitude in terms
of a Christian concept of sin and forgiveness. We believe
that we are chosen because we are loved, but that this in itself
places certain responsibilities upon us. God's forgiveness is
freely given, but exposure to such burning love makes us
more aware of sin. Most of us have experienced this in the
human sphere at some stage, when we have looked into
the eyes of someone who loves us and believes in us, and
have longed to be more worthy of that love and trust.

It was in response to the perception that they were loved
and chosen by God that the Israelites were able to move on
into a business-like relationship with their God which was
expressed in terms of a covenant. The covenant relationship
that the Jews had with God became one of the foundation
stones on which Christian theology, with its imagery of Jesus
Christ as the new covenant, was built.

Covenant

Priesthood had no place in the original formulation of the old covenant, but followed later to cope with humanity's failure to keep their side of the bargain. Gradually it was assumed that only priests could offer the necessary sacrifices that would put humanity back in right relationship with God. With the growth of an understanding that saw Christ's death and resurrection as the one perfect atonement for sin, valid for all people and all time, the Old Testament concept of priesthood was rendered obsolete; for Jesus Christ himself is the sacrifice that seals the new Covenant and brings us into right relationship with God.

Covenant is an important part of the Judaeo-Christian understanding of God and there are several attempts in the early writings to suggest that the relationship between God and the human race is based on mutual responsibility. The story of God's command to Adam and Eve that they should abstain from eating the fruit of the tree of knowledge of good and evil is not a true example of a covenant, since nothing is offered on God's side in return. 'Do and live; eat and die' reinforces a relationship of subordination based on threat, rather than responsible partnership built on promise.

A primitive form of covenant occurs twice in the story of Noah (Gen. 6:18 and 9:8). Before the flood, God makes a deal with Noah that he should build the ark and take on board a breeding couple of every species of animal, plus the wherewithal to keep all alive; and in return they shall survive the flood. After the flood, God promises that the terrors through which the people have just passed will not be repeated, and a rainbow is cast over the earth as a sign of this promise. However in this instance nothing is demanded in return, presumably because Noah has already fulfilled his part of the bargain.

This story shows the dawning of an understanding that the world works according to certain rules and pre-supposes that humanity must bear some of the responsibility for what happens to the earth. This indicates a basic grasp of the law of consequence: that it is part of the nature of how the world is that there can be no action without reaction. The fact that humanity is still struggling to learn this principle now, particularly in regard to ecological issues, is an indication of the sophistication of the religious sensibility that arose amongst the Semitic peoples of the ancient Near East.

However, the covenant that forms the basis of the Jewish religion is that described in Genesis 17. As with other covenants between God and humanity, the terms are offered by God, not by Abram, whose part in the drama is not to bargain but to discern the purposes of God and to respond. The first covenant consists of three promises made by God to Abram and three demands made of Abram in return. The three promises are

1. that God will be the God of Abram's people;
2. that Abram will give birth to a great nation; and
3. that God will bless this nation and give them the land in which they are immigrants.

In return God demands

1. that Abram's family should identify themselves as God's people, and change their names as a sign of this, Abram becoming Abraham and Sarai Sarah;
2. that all the males of the tribe should be circumcised – again as a sign; and
3. that they should have faith in God, be aware of the presence of God and strive to become perfect.

The covenant story ends with Abraham's response which is first to laugh at the promise that he would have a son, and then to obey God's command by organising a mass circumcision.

Although the story of the forming of this covenant is formulated in terms of a deal, no great issue is made of the individual elements. This is not the point at which laws are revealed, not even the Ten Commandments. God is not reported as declaring 'you must obey my commandments', but simply as advocating an insignificant physical mark, circumcision, which was in any case adopted by many people as an aid to cleanliness and health. It is almost as though it really did not matter what the sign was, as long as it was something clearly identifiable. Other forms of ritualistic cleansing, such as hand-washing, are similarly concerned with important truths that bear little relation to such physical factors as how clean or dirty one's hands are.

To a woman, the Jewish and Pauline obsession with circumcision tends to be viewed as a curious male fetish, and is certainly not one with which many of us can or should identify; but, quite apart from the practical issues of hygiene, circumcision was evidently a powerful symbol for the Jews. The New Testament writers were later to bring out its symbolic nature, but an understanding that what is intended is a circumcision of the heart is already apparent in these earliest documents. So, for instance, when the Mosaic Law is imparted, God is related as declaring: 'Yahweh your God will circumcise your heart and the heart of your descendants, until you love Yahweh your God with all your heart and soul, and so have life' (Deut. 30:6). In other words, what God is perceived as demanding is that we should be in right relationship and live in harmony with the way the world is.

> Look, to Yahweh your God belong heaven and the heaven of heavens, the earth and everything on it; yet it was on your ancestors, for love of them, that Yahweh set his heart to love them, and he chose their descendants after them, you yourselves, out of all nations, up to the present day. Circumcise your heart then and be obstinate no longer. (Deut. 10:14–17)

So first and foremost, the Law was intended to be the law of life. Its purpose is to free rather than to repress humanity and its precepts should be accepted by human beings as obvious, natural, divinely right. What is dimly discerned in the story of Abram is developed in relation to Moses, when God reassures the chosen people that 'the Word is very near to you, it is in your mouth and in your heart for your observance' (Deut. 30:14). Through the ages, God pleads with humanity that they should lay hold on life and accept the richness that is on offer. As we have seen, part of the vital truth behind the notion of the Jews being chosen is that they were not particularly good or holy, they made as many mistakes as anyone else and frequently got the wrong end of the stick. They represent humanity, and the message they bear is that they (and all humanity) are loved and valued.

The offer of life in the Gospel, 'I have come so that they may have life, and have it to the full' (John 10:10) is part and parcel of the same covenant as that forged with Moses when God declared: 'I set before you life or death, blessing or curse. Choose life, then, so that you and your descendants may live, in the love of Yahweh your God, obeying his voice, clinging to him; for in this your life consists' (Deut. 30:19–20). The nature of the world just happens to be that it works to live in certain ways and not in others.

The covenant is often referred to as though it were one single event and promise, whereas it would be more accurate to describe it in terms of the growing relationship in which the human race gradually gained insight into what was required of them by God. It grew naturally and inevitably out of their sense of being chosen by God.

Abram, or Abraham as he then became, accepted the covenant offered by God; but that was the start of the relationship rather than the culmination. In this respect the covenant resembles a human relationship like marriage, which dies if understood as a grim sticking to a once-stated contract, but becomes a living sacrament when interpreted in terms of two people learning that they affect each other and that their relationship grows, changes or dies depending on the love, faithfulness, trust and responsibilities of both.

Covenant agreed by all

Although this covenant relationship was entered into by Abram, it had to be ratified by all the people since all the people were called to be in relationship with God. So, for instance, in Exodus 24 we read of Moses making sure that the people of Israel agree to the covenant. He is then in a position to explore more closely what living in relationship with God might mean, and thus receives the Law and Commandments. The covenant is sealed in blood, with Moses sacrificing an animal and sprinkling its blood – half on the altar and half over the people. The primitive symbolism of blood, signifying the life-force, carried the same weighty resonances for the Jews as for other ancient religious people; and the theme was picked up and developed by New Testament writers in regard to the blood of Christ shed in sacrifice. The other element of life, *breath*, similarly plays a vital role in religious thought both before and after Christ, with the *ruah*, or breath of God, signifying the Holy Spirit which was later, at Pentecost, to inspire and enliven all the Church.[2]

In the same way that Moses seeks confirmation from the people that they are prepared to ratify the covenant, so Joshua invites the people to vote for God in order to show that the covenant has been freely chosen by them all (Josh. 24.14ff). The prophets, too, plead with the nation again and again to return to the purity and commitment of this initial covenant with God, reminding them of the original terms of the agreement into which they had entered. Throughout Scripture, whenever the people become forgetful or take their good fortune for granted they are forcibly reminded of the conditional nature of the covenant. For example, in Deuteronomy 29 we find Moses reminding the people that God's promises have been kept all through their wanderings; and he reiterates how vital it is that they fulfil their promises in return, through the way in which they live their lives: 'Keep the words of this covenant, put them into practice, and you will thrive in everything you do' (Deut. 29:8). It is also spelled out to them that if they fail to keep their side of the bargain, then they will perish (Deut. 8:19–20).

As the covenant relationship of the people with God grew and developed there was a gradual realisation of its implications. This is spelled out in Leviticus 26:3f: Israel's side of the deal is to live morally, keeping God's laws; God's side is to guarantee the normal rules of nature, and to ensure the success of the chosen people as a nation, so that they can 'walk with head held high'. For the point of the covenant relationship is to perceive how the world really is; to recognise the hand of God in the events of the world; and to work with, rather than against, the divine design. It is not that the benefits that accrue to the Israelites are not available to other nations, but that it is incumbent on this chosen race to recognise how good their life is and attribute it to God rather than to good fortune. This is not so very far removed from the Christian habit of saying grace before meals, inherited from the Jewish recitation of psalms before a meal. We thank God for our food, not because we fear that we would not otherwise receive it, but to express our genuine appreciation and gratitude for all that we receive.

So although the covenant is expressed in primitive terms, suggesting a rather moody God who demands tit for tat, it embodies the truth of the deepest religious sentiment that has been revealed to humanity, namely that the world is created to be good and that it is possible for humanity to live in harmony with the divine intention. Despite all the later embellishment, the whole nature of the covenant relationship is summed up in Genesis 17:2: ' "Live in my presence, be perfect, and I shall grant a covenant between myself and you, and make you very numerous." And Abram bowed to the ground.'

It is the same truth that is being probed for in the earliest creation stories, which tell of humanity created to share a perfect world, whose order and balance can only be maintained if people recognise their dependence on God, responding in humility and living in an attitude of loving gratitude. Not just the story of the Fall, but the whole history and literature of the religious people recorded in our Scriptures, bear witness to our human tendency to forget our side of the bargain when things are going well; and they remind us that we, too, have a responsibility for creating the sort of world that works according to divine laws.

The dream of a new covenant

The biblical record is a collection of meditations and revelations, first embedded in the spoken tradition and later in literature, by many people over thousands of years, all recog-

nising that life only works when we are in right relationship
with God. The covenant has priority over the Law because
it states the bottom line in terms of how the created order
is meant to be. It is only because we fail to live a perfect life
that we introduce laws; not just in relation to God, but in
human relationships too. St Augustine was later to state
another form of this initial covenant in his precept *Ama et
fac quod vis* (Love and do what you like), and unfortunately
the Christian Church has in general had no more faith
in the efficacy of this principle than the Israelites had in their
divine covenant with God.

The more the covenant was broken, the more necessary
it was to introduce rules to govern behaviour. So instead of
living in harmony with God, the Israelites evolved a sophisticated system of laws that might maximise their chances of
achieving the kind of life that would have followed if they
had lived in close relationship with God. The ten commandments form the basis for life in a civilised society; but as the
moral code became more complicated, rules and regulations
proliferated in such a way that the original simplicity of the
idea of covenant was lost.

As the observance of the Law took precedence over direct
relationship with God, there necessarily emerged a professional class whose task it was to understand and interpret
the law, to ensure that all people were subject to the law,
and to be responsible for taking away the guilt of people
when they had failed to observe the law. Thus it was the
failure of the covenant and the *growth of the Law* that brought
about the necessity for a class of priests whose job was to
interpret and enforce the covenant for the people.

The prophets called people back to the covenant not to
the Law; and in their longing for life to be governed by the
will of God they began to look forward to a fresh start, in
which a new covenant would replace the initial covenant that
had been broken both in spirit and in practice.

> See, the days are coming – it is Yahweh who speaks –
> when I will make a new covenant with the House of Israel
> (and the House of Judah), but not a covenant like the one

I made with their ancestors on the day I took them by the hand to bring them out of the land of Egypt. They broke that covenant of mine, so I had to show them who was master. It is Yahweh who speaks. No, this is the covenant I will make with the House of Israel when those days arrive – it is Yahweh who speaks. Deep within them I will plant my Law, writing it on their hearts. Then I will be their God and they shall be my people. There will be no further need for neighbour to try to teach neighbour, or brother to say to brother, 'Learn to know Yahweh!' No, they will all know me, the least no less than the greatest – it is Yahweh who speaks – since I will forgive their iniquity and never call their sin to mind. (Jer. 31:31–4)

This passage was later to be quoted in its entirety by the author of the Epistle to the Hebrews, who adds: 'By speaking of a *new* covenant, he implies that the first one is old. And anything old and ageing is ready to disappear' (Heb. 8:7–13). We shall examine in chapter 6 the way in which this Old Testament concept is developed in New Testament theology.

We have seen that as the primitive tribes of Israel grew into a nation, the formulation of rules for the order of society was elevated into a divine Law. The more complicated this Law became, the more inevitable it was that people would fail to observe it in all its detail, and the more necessary a priestly class became. Paul was later to argue that the law and perfection cannot go together, simply because the Law makes sinners out of those who fail, and this is one of the recurring themes in the Letter to the Romans.

In this way, the Law was responsible for the estrangement of the people from God. By superseding the Law, Jesus Christ brought back into focus the possibility that had been there all along, of a direct relationship between the people and God. The gospels, therefore, present a picture of a fresh start in life, in which Law and priesthood are irrelevant for those who, through the new covenant, are put back into relationship with God.

'Chosenness' and 'covenant' are two of the key concepts that New Testament Jewish writers later took from their religious history and wove into their Christology. In the Old Testament they are inextricably linked, for the Israelites are chosen to enter into covenant relationship with God: 'So now, if you are really prepared to obey me and keep my covenant, you, out of all peoples, shall be my personal possession, for the whole world is mine. For me you shall be a kingdom of priests, a holy nation' (Exod. 19:5–6).

From the dawn of history to the present day, deep within the religious consciousness of religious Jews is the understanding that if they live in close and loving relationship with God, there is no need for intermediaries. In the same way as the covenant is for *all* the people, and therefore responsible relationship with God is the privilege and duty of all, so also *the whole people* are chosen by God; and since they are chosen to be a nation of priests, there is no need or place for a professional religious class.

It is this theme that the writer of the first letter of Peter was later to pick up in encouraging the early Christians to take their common priesthood seriously, and that forms the basis of the doctrine of the priesthood of all believers. 'You are a chosen race, a royal priesthood, a consecrated nation, a people set apart to sing the praises of God who called you out of the darkness into his wonderful light' (2:9).

3

Priests and prophets

Although the belief that they were a chosen people was of paramount importance to the ancient Jews, and was the basis on which they were to build their covenant relationship with God, it was never interpreted in an individualistic sense. It was the whole race that was the chosen people, and membership of that race conferred certain privileges and responsibilities. To be chosen by God and invited to live in covenant relationship with God, made them a consecrated nation; and whatever happened to the initial pure idea as Judaism developed into a sophisticated religious system with a religious élite, their fundamental understanding of the purpose for which God had chosen them was that they were called to be a nation of priests. Right from the start, our religious heritage through Judaism includes the concept of the priesthood of all believers. 'I will count you a kingdom of priests, a consecrated nation' (Exod. 19.6).

It was as this corporate concept of priesthood gave way to a separate class of people known *individually* as priests that problems arose. The vision, however, lived on; and years later Isaiah, addressing a nation that had become a broken people, reiterates God's promise to the whole people of a new covenant in which the nation will be blessed: 'You will be called "priests of Yahweh" and be addressed as "ministers of our God" ' (Isa. 61.6).

Development of priesthood

In the stories of the covenant God made with Abraham, and the ten commandments that were entrusted to Moses on Mount Sinai, there was no mention of the investiture of priests. However, many of the races that surrounded Israel had established priesthoods, and it is not particularly surprising that as the Jewish religion developed, the possibility of a professional religious class should arise.

Only as the Israelites came into contact with different cultures, therefore, do we find the development of the concept of priesthood. In Exodus 18 we read of Moses' encounter with Jethro, his father-in-law, who was a priest from Midian and not, therefore, one of the children of Israel. On learning Israel's story, Jethro has no problem in offering sacrifice to the God of Moses, with whom his relationship is evidently warm. It was Jethro who suggested that Moses should appoint judges and evolve a delegating system of leadership, which illustrates the ease with which Israel accepted outside influence. Jethro returned to his own country, but he left his mark on the people of Israel through his encounter with Moses.

In the earliest records priests play no part in the interaction between the people and the God they worshipped, though various actions were undertaken by the father of the family or patriarch of the tribe on behalf of his community. One of the earliest functions associated with priesthood is the offering of sacrifices to God. Until the formulation of the Mosaic law, this was generally the prerogative of the firstborn son, although in the case of the earliest recorded sacrifices – those of Cain and Abel – not only did both sons offer the first fruits of their labour, but the sacrifice that was said to be favoured by God was that offered by the younger son, Abel (Gen. 4:3–5).

The early Israelites assumed that God must share their attitude towards first born sons. So it was that the most dreadful curse they could imagine being inflicted on the Egyptians was the death of their first-born and in celebration of that tragedy and in gratitude for the deliverance of their own sons at the Passover, they consecrated all their first-born sons to God. 'Consecrate all the first-born to me, the first issue of every womb, among the sons of Israel. Whether man or beast, this is mine' (Exod. 13:1). Later, however, a special caste, the Levites, replaced the first born sons, and thus professionalised the offering of sacrifices: 'I myself have chosen the Levites from among the sons of Israel, in place of the first-born, those who open the mother's womb among the sons of Israel; these Levites therefore belong to me' (Num. 3:12). The Levites were related to the first priests, Aaron and his sons, around whom cultic activity had begun to gather; and to them Moses granted special hieratic status. But in looking at the events leading to this announcement it must be admitted that the priestly profession had a rather inauspicious start. Not only were they led astray right at the foot of the mountain of God, but their investiture was sealed in blood and vengeance. Let us look again at the closing events of the well-known story.

While Moses was on the mountain with God, acquiring not only the ten commandments but numerous other precepts for the conduct and management of society and religion, the people persuaded Aaron, who had been left in charge, to give Moses up for lost and to co-operate with them in the forging of a golden calf (Exod. 32). Aaron's understanding of his priesthood does not prevent this fall into idolatry and by the time Moses returns, Israel has thrown its covenant relationship with the one God to the winds. In fury Moses seizes the calf, burns it, then grinds it to powder which he mixes with water and forces the people to drink. Although it appears that Aaron initially capitulated readily with the Israelites' request, and indeed supervised the whole operation, faced with Moses' anger he changes his tune and puts the blame squarely on the people: 'Let not my lord's anger blaze like this. You know yourself how prone this people is to evil.' We read in verse 4 that he himself made the effigy; in reporting the incident to Moses, however, his treatment of the gold is modified to 'I threw it into the fire and out came this calf' (v. 24).

Moses then demands an act of reparation and commitment to God and when the sons of Levi rally round he sets them on to their fellow Israelites. In their zeal they massacre three thousand men and it is in reward for this extraordinary violence and bloodshed that Moses marks them out as a priestly tribe: 'Today . . . you have won yourselves investiture as priests of Yahweh at the cost, one of his son, another of his brother; and so he grants you a blessing today' (v. 29). Such massacres were not unusual amongst primitive peoples, and many years earlier Levi himself had, with his brother Simeon, wreaked a bloody massacre on the Sechemites after tricking them into circumcision. On that occasion he had gone against the will of his father Jacob in his determination to avenge the honour of his sister Dinah (Gen. 24).

The Levites thus came to replace the first-born. They received no part in the sharing out of inheritance, but nor did they have any material needs, since they were kept by the community. It was the responsibility of the Levites to serve in the Tent of Meeting, as oblates or servers, and this ministry was compulsory for any male born in the tribe of Levi. The Book of Numbers describes how they were to be presented to Yahweh, whereupon the whole community should lay hands on them. They were then set aside to perform the numerous duties associated with worship. They were responsible for the Ark of the Covenant and all the artefacts used in worship. Later they carried the Ark and were able to pronounce God's blessing.

Although they were a priestly caste, the Levites were not all priests, for priests were drawn only from the direct male descendants of Aaron. There was no sense in which people were 'called' to be priests, or chosen and trained. Priests were born, according to exactly the same rules as determine the monarchical line in many cultures. Even for those who inherited the priestly mantle there was little room for personal choice or initiative. In Leviticus 8, for example, we read of the investiture of Aaron and his sons in a ceremony of cleansing and consecration. Immediately after the lengthy process was completed, two of Aaron's sons took it upon themselves to offer fire independently of the precepts laid down by Yahweh, and they were immediately struck dead

(10:1–2). Priests were not allowed to earn or possess any-thing in their own right, but were to be kept by the people.

We read in Exodus, Leviticus and Numbers of the devel-opment of priests and Levites; and throughout this lengthy period not only were special prescriptions laid on the tribe of Levi and in particular the descendants of Aaron, but we also find the steady accruing of privilege to these groups and a growing association of priesthood with power. So on the one hand we read of special clothes, of tithes paid to the priests and their claims over the food offered to Yahweh, and on the other hand the obligation that they should adhere to strict rules. They were disqualified from office if they happened to have a disability, were not allowed to marry a non-virgin (even if she were a widow) or touch alcohol while on duty, and it was their responsibility to keep the holocaust fire alight at all times. Later, recognising some of the abuses that were current then as at any other period, Ezekiel was to castigate the unfaithful Levites and reiterate the obli-gations and privileges of priesthood (Ezek. 44:10–31).

There were problems with the priesthood from the begin-ning. Not only were two of Aaron's sons, Nadab and Abihu, exterminated for disobedience, but his other sons, Eleazar and Ithamar, also failed to keep all the rules. Such failures were seen as the responsibility of the whole community; and it was not until the ministry of Jesus that we find a change in the attitude towards adherence to written rules.

Power-seeking amongst the ordained was not unknown even in early days, and Numbers 16 tells the story of an uprising of Levites and others who considered that the priests claimed too much privilege. 'You take too much on yourselves! The whole community and all its members are consecrated and Yahweh lives among them. Why set your-selves higher than the community of Yahweh?' (v. 3) When these insurrectionists were destroyed by an act of God, other Israelites complained that Moses had brought death on the people of Yahweh, and these also were punished by plague and death. Priestly privilege was evidently closely guarded from early times, and the punishments for challenging this privilege were severe.

The investiture of priests and the setting aside of Levites created a class of lay people who were utterly excluded from priestly privilege. They were distanced from cultic practices involving the holy and so, for instance, the chrism for anointing priests could not be used on them (Exod. 30). Similarly a lay person was not allowed to eat things that were deemed holy, though in this instance 'lay' was deemed to exclude the priest's family, who were permitted to eat the special foods as though they were priests (Lev. 22). The reason Ezekiel later gives for the necessity for priests to change from their special garments when leaving the Temple was not that the sacred garments might be contaminated, but to avoid the risk of blessing the ordinary people: 'they are to remove the vestments in which they have performed the liturgy and leave them in the rooms of the Holy Place, and put on other clothes, so as not to hallow the people with their vestments' (Ezek. 44:19).

It is not surprising that murmurs arose against the priests periodically, for while times were sometimes hard for the ordinary people, any man of Aaron's family could help himself to what the laity offered to God. This brought with it the risk of indolence and gluttony, and by the time of the prophets the life-style of the priests was denounced in no uncertain terms. Even during Aaron's life-time there were protests, and the moves to quell such disloyalty resulted on occasions in the introduction of a reign of terror. By the time of the prophets, diatribes against the priests were common. Isaiah complains at both priests and prophets succumbing to drunkenness:

> Priest and prophet are reeling from strong drink,
> they are muddled with wine;
> strong drink makes them stagger,
> they totter when they are having visions,
> they stumble when they are giving judgements.
> Yes, all the tables are covered with vomit,
> not a place left clean. (28:7)

Jeremiah, too, condemns the ineffectiveness of worship in the temple, claiming that it is idolatrous, empty and unrelated to

life. His criticism is not addressed directly to the priests, but
the implication that the priests were not doing anything
about an appalling situation is clear. Hosea is more direct:

> it is you, priest, that I denounce.
> Day and night you stumble along,
> the prophet stumbling with you,
> and you are the ruin of your people.
> My people perish for want of knowledge.
> As you have rejected knowledge
> so do I reject you from my priesthood. (4:6)

And in chapter 5 he blames the priests for a whole catalogue
of wrongs. It is also noteworthy that the visions of the future
that we find in the prophets do not include mention of a
priesthood.

Time and again the priests failed to set an example to the
people or to maintain religious faith and practice in the face
of pagan influence. In 2 Kings (22 and 23) it is clear that
by the time the Book of the Law is rediscovered and Josiah
initiates his religious reforms, all had wandered away from
God, including the priests. There was corruption in the
appointment of priests, and accommodation of pagan practices within the priesthood (e.g. 2 Macc. 4).

The Deuteronomic tradition, represented by the books
from Joshua to 2 Kings, regards the priests as largely responsible for the decay that led to Israel's defeat and exile.
With this hindsight the writers represent the building of the
Temple as a development that went against the wishes of
Yahweh and that opened the way for further abuse and decay.
Solomon married the daughter of an Egyptian Pharaoh (1
Kings 3:1) and the Temple itself was of Phoenician design;
so it is not surprising that pagan elements entered the Jewish
religion at this time and influenced the development of the
priesthood.

This was the point at which the earlier Hebrew understanding of Yahweh as intimate and accessible was superseded by the pagan concept of a God who demanded
appeasement and could only be approached by professionals.
Similarly devotion to a God who was characterised by a

burning desire for justice and holiness of life was replaced by careful obedience to one who was obsessed with ritual and law.

However, as the priests became more exclusively involved with the cultic and ritual aspects of religion, prophets appeared who tried to lead the people back to holiness and respect for the law of God, and in the later books of the Old Testament attention is increasingly focused on these men and women whose costly witness persuaded the Jews to return to true religion, to be forgiven and to enter into relationship with Yahweh.

Prophets

As well as the hereditary system of priesthood that evolved as Israel came into contact with other cultures and religions, there was within Judaism from the earliest times a non-hereditary system. Seers, elders and leaders were a feature of the wandering tribes that gradually cohered as the children of Israel; and there appears to have been no distinction between religious and secular roles.

Moses discovered that it is unreasonable for all the burdens of leadership to rest on one person's shoulders, so on the advice of his father-in-law Jethro he appointed leaders to help him settle disputes (Exod. 18:13ff). Then, from another source, either relating the same development in different form or describing another part of the tradition, we read in Numbers 11 of Moses, weary with the moaning of the people, complaining to Yahweh about his work load. He is instructed to gather seventy of the elders of the people and take them to the Tent of Meeting. There Yahweh causes a portion of Moses' spirit to enter the seventy elders so that they can share some of his great administrative and managerial burden.

As these people take on some of Moses's burden and undertake to share the work, they also receive some of the charisma that enabled him to go forward with the people into exploration and discovery of what it means to be chosen and loved by God. As the elders receive this spirit, they all prophesy, and this gift of prophecy even falls on a couple of elders who did not go to the tent. It is interesting to note that Joshua, who has worked for Moses for many years, assumes that he must take it up on himself to prevent those two from prophesying, as they had been in the camp rather than the Tent of Meeting when the others received their commission. Those on the 'inside' have often sought to limit the activity of God's free Spirit ever since. Moses, however, welcomes prophecy wherever it occurs: 'If only the whole people of Yahweh were prophets, and Yahweh gave his Spirit to them all!' (Num. 11:29). Although this group of seventy elders prophesied on this one occasion, we are specifically told that they did not do so again. They were chosen to help Moses with certain tasks, but they did not thereby become prophets.

Later we read of the appointment of judges to lead the people (Judg. 2:16ff). These too were political leaders, though in an age before distinctions were drawn between sacred and secular, leading the nation was seen as part of God's work. Judges were appointed to do specific work and, at least sometimes, for a specified period of time. So we read of the two old lechers in the story of Susanna, that they were 'elderly men who had been selected from the people that year to act as judges' (Dan. 13:5).

Most societies, primitive and sophisticated, have the equivalent of seers – people who by the way they live and the wisdom of their words inspire others to seek their counsel in times of need or when important decisions have to be made. In Israel these seers who arose naturally within the community later developed into what we know as prophets. 'Formerly in Israel when a man used to go to consult God he would say, "Come, let us go to the seer", for a man who is now called a "prophet" was formerly called a "seer" ' (1 Sam. 9:9).[1]

Although the terms might vary, there appear to have been prophets of one kind or another throughout history, giving advice, speaking out against injustice and false religion, staying tuned to the will of God even when the rest of society went astray, and often bursting into ecstatic utterance or movement as a result of their close encounter with God. The ordinary Hebrew word for prophet, in fact, is *Nabi*, which is derived from the verb 'to bubble forth like a fountain'.[2]

Unlike the judges, prophets were not chosen by the people; unlike priests they did not inherit the position by birth. They were closely allied to political life, sometimes even in the pay of the king, though on other occasions prophets spoke out against the kings who had appointed them. In their more formal aspects the prophets were responsible for choosing the judges and later for anointing the kings. Prophets were not exclusive to Israel: we read, for example of Balaam the Moabite who was a prophet (Num. 22–24); and women as well as men were respected as prophets: for example Miriam (Exod. 15), Deborah (Judg. 4) and Huldah (2 Chron. 34).

This catholicity of prophecy suggests a real understanding that God the Holy Spirit chooses the right person to do the right work at the right time and this represents a clearer image of the descent of that Spirit on a person than we get from most Old Testament examples of priesthood. Sometimes it almost appears that God has no say in who will be priests, since an inflexible hereditary system has been established, whereas in the choice and calling of prophets there continues to be room for divine intervention. It is God who is believed to raise up prophets from among the people.

The greatest influence of the prophets was in the period from the mid eighth to the mid sixth century BC. In the Old Testament we have the writings of sixteen prophets: Isaiah, Jeremiah, Ezekiel and Daniel are known as the four greater prophets, then the others – Hosea, Joel, Amos, Obadiah, Jonah, Micah, Nahum, Habakkuk, Zephaniah, Haggai, Zecharaiah and Malachi – are generally called the twelve lesser prophets. But many others are referred to as prophets, including Abraham, Isaac, Jacob, Moses, Aaron, Joshua, Samuel, Nathan, David and Solomon, and a number of women who are called prophetesses. There were also people who were described as false prophets, who led the people astray. The prophet Jeremiah, who was himself the son of priestly parents, condemned both prophets and priests as godless (Jer. 23:10). He denounces the prophets of Samaria as insane and accuses those in Jerusalem of adultery, persistent lying and abetting the wicked (23:14); and the same theme recurs in Micah (3:5–8) and in I Kings (22) where about four hundred prophets give King Ahab the wrong advice and thus bring about his downfall.

Deuteronomy even contains advice on how to distinguish true from false prophecy:

> You may be privately wondering, 'How are we to tell that a prophecy does not come from Yahweh?' When a prophet speaks in the name of Yahweh and the thing does not happen and the word is not fulfilled, then it has not been said by Yahweh. The prophet has spoken presumptuously. You have nothing to fear from him. (18:21–2)

Such verification of prophecy by result would, however, leave something of a question mark over Jonah, who knew only too well what it was like to prophesy events that failed to materialise.

In early accounts, ecstasy and possession are more commonly associated with prophecy than foreknowledge. The Spirit of God could enter anyone, making them prophets even if only temporarily. One example of this occurs in I Samuel 19 where we read that everyone who entered the tents at Ramah fell into an ecstasy, including Saul (vv. 19–20). Later, as we have seen, prescience was expected of the prophets, though in general their greatest asset was probably their independence and objective analysis of the political and religious events of the day which spurred them to challenge the prevailing systems, uttering forthright judgements and challenges. None of these features, ecstasy, foreknowledge or social impact, was expected of the priests, whose sphere of action was restricted to the temple and worship.

A picture of the distinction between the hereditary priest and the prophet drawn by God emerges in the story of Eli and Samuel. Eli realises that being a priest does not excuse wickedness and in the face of the unworthy behaviour of his sons he has a strong suspicion that God will cast out and punish them and choose more suitable servants (1 Sam. 2:27–36). When this truth also dawns on the child Samuel, even though he has previously had no knowledge or awareness of God, he becomes a prophet.

Although prophets often had cause to speak out against the priests, it was not unknown for the same person to be both a priest and a prophet, as was the case with Ezekiel who was born to be a priest and called by God to be a prophet; but the two roles were very different and there was often tension between priests and prophets. For example Jeremiah 20 tells of Pashhur, the priest in charge of Temple police, punishing Jeremiah for his prophecies, and in Amos 7 we find that Amaziah the priest contrived to have Amos expelled. In self-defence Amos claims that he is not a prophet, but is simply responding to God's imperative that he should speak out to the people of Israel.

In view of the fact that it was the prophets who spoke out to guide the people into the way of God, it is somewhat surprising that the Christian Church has concentrated on the training, ordination and maintenance of priests, whose function is concerned with ritual, rather than of prophets who call and lead people to God. Priests in the Old Testament are neither leaders of society nor prophets speaking with the voice of God, but a caste of men who by virtue of birth find themselves conscripted to fulfil a wholly symbolic function that brings with it certain circumscribed duties, responsibilities and privileges.

Any study of history will reveal the truth that God raises up prophets from among the people, in response to the needs of the day. In our own time, it is still the prophets that preach, that make pronouncements to the press, that guide and direct people, that demonstrate and speak out against injustice and exploitation. In contrast, all that the priest does is to perform rites. This is not to say that the priest cannot fulfil a prophetic function, and it is certainly possible to think of priests who have done so; but that it is not part of the essential nature of priesthood to be a prophet.

Prophets are chosen by God and driven by the Holy Spirit to speak out and be the voice of God in society. Unlike the privileged priests, they are always on the side of the oppressed and poor; and they speak with the nearest to the voice of God that we can detect. Even today, the ancient utterances of the prophets that have come down to us in the pages of the Old Testament are read and understood to be the word of God; and when we do discern the voice of prophecy in our own times we ignore it at our peril.

Edward Schillebeeckx points out that it was precisely this content of prophesying and teaching which was taken up into the New Testament term 'presbyter' when some degree of institutionalisation developed in the various early Christian communities.[3] It is all the more strange that so much more emphasis has been placed on the role of priest in the Church than on prophet. While priests can be carefully selected from the ranks of those who are unlikely to challenge the institution too much, and can then be trained to perform certain rites within a church, prophets are driven by the Spirit of God and are not easily controlled.

4

Priesthood in the gospels

For centuries Christians have wondered how the life of Jesus of Nazareth relates to the grand hierarchical and legalistic structure which the Church later became. Clearly an itinerant preacher and healer with a penchant for falling out with the religious authorities cannot be easily translated into an image of the model institutionalised Christian; and most clergy, whatever their denomination, would experience extreme difficulty and embarrassment if Jesus were to opt for membership of their congregation.

Luke reveals to us something of the difficulties faced by the religious authorities of his day, in the story of the Nazareth sermon. Early in his ministry Jesus visits the synagogue at Nazareth and is invited to read from the scroll of Isaiah. Choosing a passage which could well represent a mission statement for his own ministry, Jesus read

> The spirit of the Lord is on me,
> for he has anointed me
> to bring the good news to the afflicted.
> He has sent me to proclaim liberty to captives,
> sight to the blind,
> to let the oppressed go free,
> to proclaim a year of favour from the Lord.
>
> (Luke 4:18–19)

Whether or not this can be interpreted as a call to a celebration of a jubilee year, it is clear that to apply such a passage to himself was, to say the least, provocative; and it is no wonder that both his claim to be the fulfilment of this proph-

ecy, and his identification with such a call to a radical life-
style should have caused a rumpus.

Matthew, in particular, records statements and stories in
which Jesus taught his disciples to eschew the bad example
set by the religious authorities of his day. So, for instance,
we read how Jesus denounced the scribes and Pharisees in
no uncertain terms, calling them hypocrites, blind guides
and serpents, and warning the people from following their
bad example: 'The scribes and the Pharisees occupy the
chair of Moses. You must therefore do and observe what
they tell you; but do not be guided by what they do, since
they do not practise what they preach' (Matt. 23:2–3). Even
though there is no evidence that Jesus received any more
training than any other young Jewish man of the time, he
teaches with great authority and tends to out-do the scribes
at their own game: 'his teaching made a deep impression on
the people because he taught them with authority, unlike
their own scribes' (Matt. 7.29).

It was not just recognised priests who occasioned uncom-
plimentary asides, but anyone who set themselves up as a
religious professional. Some of the most graphic images Jesus
used in his stories, that have become part of our cultural
heritage, were first introduced to describe the failure of those
whose responsibility it was to guide others. So, for instance,
on one occasion he warns that anyone whose life or teaching
is responsible for leading the young or innocent astray will
receive the most dreadful punishment imaginable (Matt.
18:5–7). He describes false prophets as ravening wolves in
sheep's clothing (7:15), and tells his hearers to judge such
people by their fruits: a test that should still be applied to
anyone holding office or responsibility in the Church (7:22).

In view of such harsh condemnations it is not surprising
that as time passed Jesus's relationship with the religious
professionals moved inexorably from strained to confron-
tational and that the Jewish leaders eventually played a significant part in causing him to be put to death. Jesus clearly
did not identify with the priests or invite them to share in
his mission.

Although the Pharisees were not for the most part drawn

from the priestly classes, and they frequently opposed the professional Sadducees, they did not represent a genuinely lay movement. They were interpreters and teachers of the Law, and as such were more closely aligned with authority than with the ordinary people who struggled to observe the various strictures laid down by such religious experts.

The choice of lay disciples

None of the gospels leave us in any doubt that the religious movement that grew up around Jesus, and which was later to develop into the Christian Church, was a lay movement. Without exception, the people Jesus chose to share his earthly ministry, to learn from him, grow in communion with him and risk everything to take his message out into the wider world were, and remained, unambiguously lay people.

There were plenty of professionals Jesus could have chosen to share his mission – Levites, priests, Sadducees, Pharisees, scribes or lawyers – and not all of these were bad or intrinsically unworthy of receiving a divine commission. For instance, John's gospel presents a fascinating little cameo of the Pharisee Nicodemus, 'a leader of the Jews', who was clearly a good man, and receptive to the message of Jesus. He listened to what Jesus had to say and meditated on it in such a way that his life was gradually changed; and he had more courage and practical love of Jesus after the crucifixion than all the core disciples whose prime concern in this time of crisis appears to have been to make themselves scarce and save their own skins.

We first meet Nicodemus visiting Jesus under cover of darkness and although on this occasion Jesus does not appear to have fallen over himself to be helpful, he did give Nicodemus the credit of being able to grasp theological concepts that were above the heads of many of his regular followers. The conversation recorded in John 3 contains, in a nutshell, Jesus's teaching on baptism and the Holy Spirit, the kingdom of God, the purpose of the crucifixion, the offer of life and nature of judgement. Whether it was given in one chunk or over a period of time, this passage constitutes one of the densest presentations of the philosophy that Jesus was expounding in his life and ministry.

So impressed and committed is Nicodemus that when the Pharisees turn nasty and begin to look for ways in which to arrest and silence Jesus, he is prepared to speak out in support of giving him a fair hearing (John 7:50–52). Like Mary Magdalen and several of the women who accompanied Jesus, Nicodemus observed and assimilated, and after the crucifixion risked his own reputation and safety by coming with Joseph of Arimathaea to give the body of Jesus a decent burial.

In similar vein Mark and Luke describe Joseph of Arimathaea as a prominent member of the Council, who had not gone along with the majority decision to dispose of Jesus (Mark 15.43; Luke 23:50–52) and whose longing to see the kingdom of God was able to accommodate the unorthodox person and teaching of Jesus of Nazareth. Later, the intervention of the Pharisee Gamaliel in the meeting of the Sanhedrin (Acts 5.34) again suggests that there were Jewish religious leaders who were on the side of the angels and who might well have provided promising material for discipleship. If this is the same Gamaliel who taught Paul how to be a Pharisee (Acts 22.3), perhaps it is not too fanciful to suggest that we owe to him some part of the religious foundation that was later to develop Christian doctrine and theology and spread it around the whole of the known world.

In view of the fact that such good Jewish professionals were available, it is noteworthy that Jesus chose a group of disciples who were exclusively lay. In describing the love that is meant to be the hallmark of Christian discipleship, Jesus reminded his followers that they were not a self-selected group, but were chosen by him for a specific function – namely to go out into the world and bear fruit. What one does not know, of course, and is never likely to know, is how many others were called who did not respond to the invitation.

Training of the twelve

Much has been made in the Church of the position of these twelve men, though it is impossible to be sure that their pre-eminence is anything other than a reading back into history of the structures that developed in the early Church. It does not take much imagination to understand how some of the early Jewish Christians would have sought signs and symbols to represent the new movement as a fulfilment and mirror of the old religion. Twelve male disciples translates neatly back into the twelve tribes of Israel and has the merit that as long as Jesus had at least twelve close associates, twelve of them could be picked out for special mention.

Even in the matter of naming the twelve, there is some inconsistency between the various traditions represented in the different gospels. John names only four disciples, one of whom (Nathanael) does not occur in any of the other sources. Thadaeus occurs only in Matthew and Mark; and Judas (or Jude in Acts) the son of James, is included in the Luke-Acts narratives. The followers of Jesus, then as now, are generally known as his disciples, and the group of close friends that accompanied Jesus might well have changed from time to time. Both Matthew and John describe Joseph of Arimathea as a disciple; and John uses the word to refer also to the man born blind (John 9:38), and records Jesus describing all who believe in him as his disciples (8.31).

The gospels tell us little or nothing about most of the men reported to have been the disciples of Jesus. Even in the closing words of St Matthew's gospel, in which Jesus, follow-ing the resurrection, sends his disciples out into the world to continue his mission, there is no differentiation between the status of the eleven surviving disciples and those who will in future become disciples through their evangelism. So Matthew 28:16 speaks of the eleven *disciples* setting out for Galilee to meet Jesus, and then describes his commission to them as being to 'make *disciples* of all nations'.

The first appearances of the risen Lord were to women and to an otherwise unknown couple walking home to Emmaus. In each case these people are given a commission by Jesus, even though they had not been included in the calling of the twelve. *These* are the first apostles of Jesus Christ, sent to tell of his resurrection; not the group of twelve who were still huddled in hiding in the upper room.

Later, after Pentecost, other disciples are also sent out into the world and although this larger group is not in the privileged position of the first disciples, with the rhythm of spending time with Jesus and going out to the world, they are clearly expected to carry with them an awareness of the presence of Jesus at all times. They were to share in his life, his dying and his resurrection, perhaps in a way that was not possible for those first friends who shared the life of an unknown itinerant preacher around Galilee. What is more, they were sent out to baptise, not to ordain. Making priests was quite definitely not part of their remit.

There are clear indications in the gospels that the original group of twelve disciples was not meant to form an exclusive club. For instance, when some of these disciples show signs of wanting to exercise control over others and come to Jesus for approval, they are disappointed.

John said to him, 'Master, we saw someone who is not one of us driving out devils in your name, and because he was not one of us we tried to stop him.' But Jesus said, 'You must not stop him; no one who works a miracle in my name could soon afterwards speak evil of me. Anyone who is not against us is for us.' (Mark 9.38–40)

This passage occurs in Mark immediately after the scene in which Jesus has responded to the disciples' squabbles as to which of them is the greatest, by setting a child among them as an example of the truly great. In the next chapter we read of ambition raising its head again, when James and John try to stake their claim to be *primus inter pares* and the other disciples respond with indignation.

In Matthew's gospel (20:20) the request comes from the mother of the brothers, but the rest of the group still blames her sons for the aspirations to greatness, and Jesus's response is identical. This time the model of greatness he offers them is embodied in the figure of a slave, and the only honour they are promised is suffering. It is strange indeed that in subsequent church history so much has been made of apostolic succession and so little of this description of the true disciple as the suffering slave. We shall see, in chapter 12, that suffering can, indeed, be seen as one of the prime elements of priesthood.

It would appear, then, that for much of the time the disciples played no special part in relation to the other followers of Jesus and were expressly discouraged from assuming any special status. Sometimes disciples were given specific practical tasks to do, such as preparing for the Passover meal, and on occasions Jesus would eat with the twelve. But teaching and example were taken from Jesus alone and rather than forming a close-knit exclusive community, the movement that grew up around Jesus was remarkable for the way in which it was open to women, Samaritans, gentiles and the untouchables of society. What we see in the gospels is not a hierarchy, but a rather loose and flexible circle with Jesus at the centre.

The gospel narratives even suggest that some of the most important theological expositions Jesus gave were not to his disciples, but to such outsiders as Nicodemus (John 3), the woman at the well (John 4) or a group of Greek sightseers who happened to be around at festival time (John 12.20 ff). The disciples in general show no exceptional aptitude for grasping the point of Jesus's teaching: they have to have the significance and meaning of the parable of the sower spelled out to them (Luke 8:4–15), they fail, even after long hours and months in the company of Jesus, to understand the cost of discipleship (Luke 18.28–34); and are so thrown off balance by observing the transfiguration that Peter immediately tries, nervously, to trivialise the experience (Matt. 17:4; Mark 9.5; Luke 9:33). Nor do they in general show exceptional faith; and their panic in the storm, or their baffled failure when faced with a boy with epilepsy, do not compare well with the great faith shown by the centurion whose servant was dying or the woman seeking a cure for her daughter.

The picture one is given of Jesus's disciples is not one of

an embryonic seminary, with bright young men learning to be the theologians of tomorrow; but rather of a motley group of friends who bear the responsibility for getting on with the practical jobs that have to be done, such as keeping order when the crowd grows too large for comfort (Mark 6.35–40), introducing enquirers to Jesus (John 12:20–22), providing food for the company (John 4:8) or organising the Passover meal (Matt. 21:1). These practical, unromantic tasks are the model on which the Church was built, but, strangely, they are not the sort of qualifications that appear in most clerical job descriptions or CVs.

However, whether 'the twelve' relates to the inner circle of Jesus's acquaintances or to the structures of the early Church, it is impossible to ignore the theological significance of the choice of these very ordinary people as disciples; for it clearly mirrors the choice by God of the Jewish nation to receive the divine covenant. To seek an honest perception of and response to the real identity and role of the disciples in the gospels in no way detracts from the important part they played in the earthly ministry and mission of Jesus or diminishes the dynamic and life-enhancing consequences of spending three years in close physical proximity to him. In the Acts of the Apostles, Luke presents us with a picture of the way in which some of these ordinary people developed as they discovered the Spirit of God working in and through them as they carried the message of Jesus Christ out into the wider world. The changes that can result from living in the knowledge of the presence of God can still be observed in the lives and faces of ordinary people that we meet and know: how much more apparent this must have been in those whose lives were touched by God in human form.

It would be easy to argue that Jesus did not envisage a system of Christian priesthood, but then he almost certainly did not envisage the setting up of the Christian Church. It would, however, appear that Jesus was conscious of training his disciples up to an awareness and reliability that would enable them to preserve and disseminate his message when he was no longer present in the flesh. One is aware of this task becoming more urgent with the passage of time, and of the exasperation Jesus sometimes felt and expressed that his teaching had not been understood or assimilated into the disciples' lives.

One of the most powerful training exercises recorded in the gospels is the washing of the disciples feet which takes the place of the institution of the Eucharist in St John's gospel (ch. 13). John describes Jesus at this point as being fully aware of his relationship with God and of the urgency, in the light of his forthcoming death, to pass on the essentials of his mission to those he will leave behind. Although it is widely claimed that Jesus was a moral teacher there are in fact very few clear injunctions in the gospels. It is tempting to add that this is just as well, since the Church has consistently and shamelessly broken the few commands of Christ that are reported. One of these occurs when he has washed the feet of each of his disciples and then, returning to the table and addressing them directly, he tells them that they are to wash one another's feet. Whether this is meant literally or metaphorically, the practice has been more honoured in its breach than its observance among those who lay claim to being the successors of these first disciples.

Another clear directive Jesus is reported as having given but which has consistently been broken relates to the forms of address by which religious leaders should be known:

> You . . . must not allow yourselves to be called Rabbi, since you have only one Master, and you are all brothers. You must call no one on earth your father, since you have only one Father, and he is in heaven. Nor must you allow yourselves to be called teachers, for you have only one Teacher, the Christ. The greatest among you must be your servant. (Matt. 23.8–11)

In the face of such a clear directive, it is strange indeed that some parts of the Church have encouraged the laity to call their clergy 'father'.

More understandable in terms of the practicalities of life, but no more permissible according to directives given by Jesus, is the practice of accepting remuneration for Christian ministry. For when Jesus commissions the disciples and sends them out as apostles, he specifically instructs them that, though it is reasonable to accept hospitality from those to whom they minister, they should not charge for the work they do: 'You received without charge, give without charge'. (Matt. 10.8). If this injunction had been obeyed, it is unlikely that there would have been so many ordinations throughout history.

These hints and guesses found in the gospels can not, of course, give anything approaching a blueprint for what Jesus Christ intended any organised form of Christian ministry to be. But on the other hand they do give us a reasonably clear impression of what it was meant *not* to be, and some aspects of this picture bear uncomfortable resemblances to what it subsequently became.

So we have the picture of a lay man, gathering around him a group drawn exclusively from the laity and training them to overturn the normal political and religious expectations of society. He trains them to humility and suffering and sends them out to carry the message to whoever is willing to hear it. He confronts the religious authorities and refuses to back down; he works with and for ordinary people and teaches them not only to pray, but to relate directly and intimately to God rather than relying on professionals; and he tells rattling good stories, some of which have a decidedly anti-clerical twist.

Jesus's attitude towards the clergy

Matthew (ch. 23) records one sustained and fairly virulent attack by Jesus on the scribes and Pharisees. Whether or not all these criticisms were made on one occasion or were a recurring theme of his teaching is immaterial: they were clearly common enough to be symptomatic of Jesus's general attitude to the religious leaders. In this chapter, Jesus describes the scribes and Pharisees in no uncertain terms as hypocrites who lead others astray; and the vituperative metaphors follow each other in quick succession: blind guides, whitewashed tombs, serpents, brood of vipers.

On other occasions, however, humour rather than invective, was the weapon Jesus used to castigate the respected religious leaders of his day. One of the most widely-known and best-loved of such stories is, of course, the parable of the Good Samaritan (Luke 10.33). In this example Jesus takes both a priest and a Levite, the two different forms of religious élite, and sets them up as 'fall guys'. When they have failed to come to the aid of the poor victim of mugging, a Samaritan – the stereotype of the most unrespected and despised in society – behaves in the godly and practical manner that the occasion demands. Although priest and Levite are shown in such a bad light, neither acts out of character or does anything of which they themselves would be ashamed; for as devout Jews their prime concern was to maintain their ritual purity, and if they had touched the man and found that he really was dead, they would have been deemed unclean and prevented from taking part in their religious rituals.

Despite the roles in which Jesus casts the priest and Levite, the telling of this story is not an opportunity for Jesus to vent his spleen on the religious leaders who persecuted him, but is, rather, the presentation of a critique of the danger of the whole Law to which they subscribed. The major sin of priest and Levite was not that they acted without compassion but that they adhered to the Law when a higher Law demanded that they should break it. Having said that, the spicy attraction of this part of the story to those who first heard it would have been precisely that it cut the clergy down to size. As Jesus pointed out on another occasion (Matt. 23:6), the clergy were all too ready to take seats of honour and to bask in their privileged positions.

The other important example of clerical stereotyping by Jesus occurs not in a parable but in the Johannine discourses (John 10.12). Jesus describes himself as the good shepherd and contrasts his loving care for the sheep with the lack of practical concern exhibited by an 'hireling', someone who is paid to look after someone else's sheep. How many congre-

gations throughout history, disappointed at the apparent lack
of true pastoral or spiritual concern demonstrated by their
clergy, have heard the description of the hireling shepherd
and smiled wryly as they picked up the subtle significance
of the imagery?

I am the good shepherd:
the good shepherd lays down his life for his sheep.
The hired man, since he is not the shepherd
and the sheep do not belong to him,
abandons the sheep
as soon as he sees a wolf coming, and runs away,
and then the wolf attacks and scatters the sheep;
he runs away because he is only a hired man
and has no concern for the sheep.

At no time did Jesus claim priesthood. It is clear from
Matthew's genealogy that he did not belong to the tribe of
Aaron and therefore could not, within a Jewish context, bear
priestly status; but he would have been widely accepted as a
prophet and in his rejection and death he met a prophet's
end. In the gospel story it is the religious leaders who are
largely responsible for condemning Jesus to death, and as
we have seen, he was not averse to criticising them or sending
them up in his stories and other teachings.

We saw in the last chapter how the prophets who challenged the people to return to responsible theocentric citi-
zenship spoke of the dream of a new covenant with God, in
harmony with the first covenant in which the nation was
chosen to be a priestly people. As the writers of the early
Church began to interpret the life, death and resurrection
of Jesus Christ, they came to see the Christ-event as the
pivotal point of history, in which the earliest and purest
religious perceptions of the Jewish people are re-affirmed
and reinterpreted to include all races among the chosen
people. As in the original understanding, this involves a
personal commitment to and relationship with God by the
people, which dispenses with the need for intermediaries.

We shall see later how religious history repeated itself: for
in the same way that the purity of vision represented in the

covenant was gradually overlaid by tribal competition, cultic practices and the development of a priestly caste system, so the Church, as it grew and developed, once again lost the initial inspiration as it found new ways in which to institutionalise the faith and bring it under the equivalent of the Law.

5

Leadership in the early Church

As the gospels do not contain directives for the formation of a professional Christian ministry, an appeal to the practice of the early Church is the next most likely source for guidance. Unfortunately, however, the picture that emerges from the Acts of the Apostles and the New Testament letters serves to confuse, rather than clarify the situation.

It is undeniable that there were privileged positions and unedifying power struggles in the early Church; but nothing resembling an hieratic priesthood emerges in the Acts of the Apostles or the early letters of Paul. It would never have occurred to the early Jewish-Christian community which, according to Acts continued for some time to worship in the Temple, to initiate an alternative system of Christian priesthood based on Jewish models.

It must be borne in mind that the word 'priest' is never used in the New Testament to refer to someone engaged in Christian ministry. There are, of course, references to Jewish priests, but the introduction of the term into the terminology of the Christian Church is later than any of the canonical writings. The concept of priesthood, as far as Christian writers were concerned, was used *either* to refer to the sacerdotal activity of Jesus Christ our great high priest, *or* to describe the whole body of Christian people – the priesthood of all believers; never to describe individuals or office within the Church.

One reason for this is offered by Michael Ramsey, in *The Christian Priest Today*, when he writes:

In the books of the New Testament the title priest is never

given to the ministry: apostles or bishops or presbyters are never called priests. If they had been so described in the early days of Christianity, it might have suggested a kind of continuation of the Levitical priests of the old covenant, and that old order had been totally superseded by the new concept of priesthood in the person of Christ himself. Indeed, in the New Testament there are two uses of the word priest in relation to Christianity: Jesus Christ himself is priest, and the whole Church is a priesthood.[1]

Added to this is the fact that all early Christians were keyed up and waiting for the Parousia, which they believed was imminent. With the return of Jesus Christ expected any day there was little point in evolving structures or developing a strategy for appointing intermediaries or leaders. All that was necessary was to muddle along, all sharing the excitement and responsibilities, until Christ returned to gather everything in to the commonwealth of God.

The pattern of the early Church that emerges in the Acts of the Apostles, therefore, is of a community of believers, learning, breaking bread and praying together. Although initially a community of Jewish people who continued their allegiance to the temple, there was a commonality in worship – which took place in people's homes – that was a reflection of the commonality in material goods by which they made sure that none of their number was in need. While the eschatological hope was urgent, there was no need for structures and hierarchies which in any case ran counter to the teaching of Jesus. These were introduced later, presumably to help to keep hope alive with the passage of time.

Ministering to the first communities

As the months slipped into years and the years into decades with no sign of the return of Jesus Christ, the Church continued to grow and spread far beyond the Jerusalem community and some organisation and structure became necessary and desirable. By the end of the second century there are clear signs of the beginning of a three part ministry of bishop, presbyters and deacons, on which most later church order is built. Bishops were the guardians of the faith, and were probably the most numerous group; presbyters were the elders, or respected members of Christian society; and much of the work of the Church was done by deacons, a word that, like minister, suggests humble service, since *diakonos* is a servant, or one who waits at table.

All these groups were chosen by the local congregations and would have been seen as representative of the people of that locality, rather than being imposed from without; and none of them would have been called priests. It is only in the third century, for example in the Ordinal of Hippolytus and the writings of Cyprian and Tertullian, that the word 'priest' begins to be used in a Christian context, first to denote a bishop, and then for presbyters as well.

However, long before this time leaders emerged in the churches, and people with different gifts were appointed to serve in various ways. Separate traditions began to emerge in the Christian communities, depending on such factors as geographical locality, original religious affiliation and the identity of the founding apostle.

If the first Christians had set out to found a Church they would have planned an institution with more uniformity of structure and office than the rather amorphous mass of communities that emerged during the early years of Christianity. But these were not trained leaders planning an institution to last through into the second or third millennium and beyond, but ordinary people gripped by the excitement of a new consciousness and life style, expecting any day to witness the return of Jesus Christ and the birth of a new order. Some had been changed dramatically by personal contact with Jesus; for others their centre of gravity had been radically shifted by the experience of Pentecost or the enthusiasm of those who carried that charismatic experience out into the wider world. We read in Acts that the events of Pentecost were witnessed by people from all over the known world: 'Parthians, Medes and Elamites; people from Mesopotamia, Judaea and parts of Libya round Cyrene; residents of Rome – Jews and proselytes alike – Cretans and Arabs' (Acts 2:9–11). It is hardly surprising that as these people formed or joined Christian communities and the boundaries of the Church expanded to accommodate the various experiences and traditions, very different patterns should emerge.

James Dunn undertakes to tease out some of the different strands that appear so tangled in early Christian writings, and concludes that although a number of variations are in evidence, there were two major, and fundamentally opposed, patterns of ministry that developed in the early Church.[2] One of these was associated with the Jewish Church in Jerusalem, particularly as James the brother of Jesus became prominent, and this pattern was increasingly structured along similar lines to the synagogue; while the other, represented by Paul, was more free and charismatic in character. Dunn characterises Luke as attempting an assimilation of these very different patterns in the Acts of the Apostles.

Even if this is something of a simplification, the identification of two models along the lines of Jewish and Hellenistic conversions does accord with the fact that those who, like Paul, went out to the gentiles soon diverged from the church that grew up around the brother of Jesus in Jerusalem, and would help to explain why the New Testament does not present a unified picture of ministry.

Apostles

According to the Acts of the Apostles, on the Day of Pentecost it was the apostles who assumed the initial positions of leadership and began to preach. This group consisted of Jesus's original disciples who had regrouped in Jerusalem after the resurrection, plus Matthias, the man chosen to make up their number following Judas's suicide. Apostles maintain their prime importance throughout the New Testament writings, but as time passes interpretation of who or what an apostle is becomes much more flexible. The first stories of the early Church revolve around the disciples Peter, James and John; but the importance of these first apostles diminishes, particularly as James the brother of Jesus assumes leadership of the Jerusalem church.

The election of Matthias (Acts 1:15–26), generally accepted as uncontroversial is, in fact, an astonishing little story for two reasons. First, the arbitrary nature of the election puts a strange complexion on the disciples' understanding of divine guidance, which they apparently saw as working more reliably through a lottery than through the prayer, discussion and normal decision-making processes of the group. Secondly, while it is one thing to believe that those who had been chosen by Jesus to accompany him throughout his earthly ministry should assume a special status as the new teaching spread, it is quite another to maintain the original number artificially by bringing in someone who had not been part of that group.

It is noteworthy that there was no similar replacement procedure after the death of James a few years later (Acts 12.1), even though at that time there were still probably something approaching 500 people who had witnessed the death and resurrection of Jesus Christ, and any of these could quite reasonably have been chosen to maintain the original number. The initial choice of twelve, as we have seen, mirrors the twelve tribes of Israel and would have been understood as a symbol that through these twelve everyone could be included. The preservation of this group of twelve is likely to have been important in interpreting the gospel to Jews in the early days, but as the mission was extended to the Gentiles it became less important to impose imagery from Judaism on the new converts.

The widespread belief that there were in the early Church twelve apostles who corresponded exactly to the eleven surviving disciples of Jesus with the addition of Matthias to replace Judas, does not accord with the evidence of the New Testament, which names a number of apostles who did not belong to this group. It would not even be true to say that they were all in a position to witness to their personal experience of the life, death and resurrection of Jesus Christ.

For a start, one of the most famous of the apostles of the Church is Paul, who never met the man Jesus, though it is undeniable that he had a dramatic personal encounter with the risen Christ. He refers to himself as the least of the apostles, but is in no doubt that he should be numbered among them. James the brother of Jesus came, in time, to be considered by many to be the foremost of the apostles, and by about AD 50 he was the most authoritative person in the Jerusalem Church (Acts 12:17; 15:13ff; 21:18ff), yet he was not one of Jesus's disciples and there is at least the whiff of a suggestion in the synoptic gospels that the immediate family of Jesus were not entirely in sympathy with what he was doing during his ministry (Matt. 12:46–50; Mark 3:31–5; Luke 8:19–21).

So, apart from Peter who was the first natural leader of the new community, the two major apostolic figures that emerged as the Church became established were Paul and James the brother of Jesus, neither of whom were members of the original group of twelve. It is possible that James qualified by virtue of having witnessed the resurrection; and Paul then interprets that more loosely, in effect throwing the door open to all who later came to experience resurrection in a vivid spiritual way:

> . . . he was raised to life, in accordance with the scriptures, and that he appeared to Cephas; and later to the Twelve; and next he appeared to more than five hundred of the brothers at the same time, most of whom are still with us, though some have fallen asleep; then he appeared to James, and then to all the apostles. Last of all he appeared to me too, as though I was a child born abnormally. (1 Cor. 15:5–8)

According to this passage it would appear, first, that the twelve and the five hundred are considered by Paul to be sub-groups of the apostles; and secondly that Paul, at this stage, does not claim apostleship for himself.

Another definition of an apostle is 'one who is sent', and this, of course, can include a great many more people; though it then becomes more difficult to say who, among the converted, is *not* an apostle. In any case, if an apostle is one who witnessed the life, death and resurrection of Jesus

Christ, and/or who is sent to bear witness to the resurrection, then the prime candidate for apostleship must certainly be Mary Magdalen, who qualifies on all counts.

Mary Magdalen appears to have been so closely associated with Jesus that some have posited the theory that she was his wife. Whether or not this is more than fancy, Mary clearly held an important position among the followers of Jesus, and she was the first to witness the resurrection and to receive a commission to tell others the good news. The gnostic writings include a gospel of Mary Magdalen; and it is at least arguable that she, rather than Peter, should have been accorded the honour of being recognised as the first and foremost of the apostles. In view of this, it is encouraging that Mary Magdalen has, in recent years, begun to be accorded more honour, as feminist theologians have drawn attention to her pre-eminence and obedient apostleship.

With the passage of time, however, other leaders emerge who are also given apostolic status, and the meaning of the word appears to stretch to include those who found new churches. Paul mentions a number of apostles by name, sometimes, as in the case of Andronicus and Junia, in deferential terms: 'Greetings to those outstanding apostles, Andronicus and Junius (or Junia) . . . who were in Christ before me' (Rom. 16:7). Other candidates for this understanding of apostleship would probably include Barnabas (Acts 14:4); Apollos (1 Cor. 1–4); Epaphroditus (Phil. 2:25); Silvanus and Timothy (1 Thess. 1:1).

Apostolic succession in the early Church should be understood as the succession of the teaching and ministry of Jesus, not as an élite club whose members had to sanction and initiate new members. It is the *word* that is passed down through these people, and that has continued to be treasured and transmitted by the Christian Church throughout history, not status. As long as the teaching of the church is 'apostolic', and is consistent with that which was received from Christ, then apostolic succession is intact: 'As for you, my dear son, take strength from the grace which is in Christ Jesus. Pass on to reliable people what you have heard from me through many witnesses, so that they in turn will be able to teach others (2 Tim. 2:1, 2).

Hans Küng, in *The Church*, argues that apostolic succession was (and is) living as witnesses to the apostolic message handed down to us from the New Testament: 'fundamentally the *whole* Church, and hence every individual member, stands in the line of succession from the apostles; provided that the Church and each individual member is concerned to be in accordance with the apostolic witness and to continue the apostolic ministry.'[3] For Küng, that means that every Christian is a true successor of the apostles, by virtue of being part of the apostolic community. He suggests that this is one of the main reasons for the rapid growth of Christianity in the early years: it was *not* dependent on professionals, but rather spread by merchants, soldiers and seafarers, all of whom were apostles of Jesus Christ, sent to make disciples of all nations.

This, of course, is the true meaning of apostolic succession. It is *not* meant to suggest a religious relay race, whereby being touched by the person who last held a baton imbues magical powers and qualities. Rather, it is the constant checking of the developing doctrine, to make sure that the Gospel, in being disseminated and reinterpreted in many different times and cultures, remains true to the purity of its original meaning and purpose.

It was precisely to ensure this consistency of teaching that in time presbyters were appointed. Their function had nothing to do with rules over who should celebrate the sacraments; but was simply to ensure uniformity of teaching, particularly when heresies started to threaten some of the fundamental aspects of the faith. They also came to play a part in encouraging the community to maintain standards of Christian behaviour.

There is no avoiding the fact that what we would now call denominationalism soon reared its head in the early Church. For instance, the Acts of the Apostles records the beginning of the division between those who remained true to Judaism and those who saw the necessity to move outside the strictures of the old religion for the sake of gentile converts.

There appear to have been at least two major factions in the early Church: the Hebrew church led initially by Peter and later by James, and the gentile church under Paul. We see from the letter to the Galatians (ch. 2) that Peter, who was drawn towards a more open approach for the sake of non-Jews, was called back into line by James, who became the dominant force in the hebraicising of the Jerusalem church. So although there was initially an amicable division of authority, with Peter concentrating on the mission to the Jews and Paul to the Gentiles (Gal. 2:7–10), it was not long before friction developed between the two leaders (2:11–14).

Diversity of gifts and ministries

One of the features of the different communities and traditions is that they evolved differing patterns of ministry and leadership. Those in positions of authority are frequently just called 'leaders', but a number of other terms are also common. The words *episkopos* and *presbyteros* appear to be practically synonymous (Acts 20:17, 28); there are teachers, prophets, pastors and evangelists (e.g., Eph. 4:11). Peter describes himself as an 'elder' (1 Pet. 5:1–4) (or *presbyteros*, which can simply imply age) and evidently expects the elders in the churches of Asia Minor to read out his letter to their congregations. But there is no mention of elders in any of Paul's letters, until we come to the Pastoral Epistles, which are most probably post-Pauline. Acts 6 records the appointment of the first deacons, which came about as a direct result of mistrust between the Hellenist and Hebrew Christian communities. In the first instance they were appointed by the community to take over some of the daily distribution of food from the apostles; but clearly the deacons did not limit themselves to the housekeeping, for we read in Acts of both Stephen and Philip being involved in preaching and evangelism (chs. 6 and 8). The earliest recorded Christian sermon is by Stephen; and Philip, by travelling to spread the message, was acting as an apostle.

The early Church was concerned with coping with differ-

ent circumstances as they arose, rather than with construct-
ing a logical pattern for ordering an institution. We therefore
find many different ministries in the churches, including
prophets, teachers, miracle-workers and others; and one of
Paul's recurring pleas to the churches is that all these various
ministries should be valued:

> To some, his gift was that they should be apostles; to
> some prophets; to some, evangelists; to some, pastors and
> teachers; to knit God's holy people together for the work
> of service to build up the Body of Christ, until we all
> reach unity in faith and knowledge of the Son of God.
> (Eph. 4:11–13)

So he emphasises again and again the importance of the
different contributions everyone has to make to the whole,
and reminds the communities that what matters is not position within the Church, but the living out of Christian love
(1 Cor. 12; Eph. 4:7; Rom. 12 etc.).

One consistent feature of the early Church that is clear,
however, is that ministers of whatever kind emerged from
within the congregations, and the authority for appointing
and commissioning them resided in the whole church, not
in officials.

> . . . this authority was regarded as collective or communal
> or organic rather than as residing in permanent
> officials . . . even when permanent official ministries
> emerge, they are . . . offices representative of and bearing
> authority delegated to them by the whole Christian
> people.[4]

This is as true of the *episkopoi* as it is of the deacons, of the
prophets as much as the teachers. They are chosen and
commissioned *because* they show aptitude for that particular
ministry. They are *not* appointed so that they can subsequently be trained to perform that function. This is an
important distinction, and is one of the reasons why, when
the system worked, there was a real sense in which all the
different ministers, of whatever kind, were called directly by
God through the operation of the Holy Spirit.

Division between ordained and lay Christians

The fact that all the functions that later became the preserve of priesthood were the responsibility of the whole community does not mean that everyone could do everything: far from it. Paul is at pains to point out that people should exercise those particular gifts that have been given to them. Nor does it mean that church worship and order were not the responsibility of individuals whose major concern it was to maintain high standards. But as far as we can see, in every case the person became a minister by being chosen by the congregation. For instance, Schillebeeckx points out that anyone who was chosen by the community to preside at the Eucharist became, *ipso facto*, a minister instituted by the Church.[5] The question, therefore, of whether or not lay Christians could celebrate the Eucharist in the early Church is virtually meaningless, since by virtue of being chosen by the community to so celebrate, the lay person assumed the necessary office to become a eucharistic minister.

This process has considerable attractions as a model for the Church today, since it allows flexibility and growth without the dangers of anarchy or disorder. Under such a system some of the convolutions and sins from which the Church later came to suffer, could not arise. Schillebeeckx extrapolates:

> the modern situation in which a community might not be able to celebrate the eucharist because no priest is present is theologically inconceivable in the early Church; the community chooses a president for itself and has hands laid on him so that they can also be a community which celebrates the eucharist, i.e. a 'community of God'. In that case the vitality of the community in terms of the gospel is the deciding factor, not the availability of a body of priestly manpower, crammed full of education in one place or another.[6]

The dangerous division of the Church into clergy and laity came much later and there is a real sense in which the early Church was a community of priests. Kenneth Stevenson has shown how the major sacrament of initiation in the early Church was baptism, which was not undertaken lightly but involved something like three years of careful preparation and learning.[7] Baptism was initiation into the full life of the Church, which meant membership of the priestly people. All baptised Christians were, and are, priests; and the fact that the Church later allowed the establishment of a professional class of ordained priests does not in any way diminish the importance or the validity of this baptismal priesthood that is shared by all.

There are plenty of references to the *laos* in the New Testament, all of which use this concept to mean the people of God as opposed to those outside the Christian community. It was certainly *not* used to differentiate a subsection of that community. Hans Küng, in *The Church*, discusses the original meaning of the term:

> It is striking that the word *laos* with the meaning 'people of God' is so often used for the Christian community, whereas the word λαϊκός, 'layman', whether in the Gentile meaning of the 'uneducated masses' or in the Jewish meaning of one who is neither priest nor Levite, simply does not occur in the New Testament . . . The word *laos* in the New Testament, as also in the Old Testament, indicates no distinction within the community as between priest ('clerics') and people ('laity'). It indicates rather the fellowship of all in a single community. The distinction it implies is one outside the community, between the whole people of God and the 'non-people', the 'world' and the 'heathens'. Not until the third century do we find any distinction between 'clerics' and 'laymen'.[8]

Bishop John Robinson, in *Layman's Church*, argues that this two-tiered system of clergy and laity in the Church was introduced almost entirely under secular influence, possibly affected by Roman ideas and practices of government.[9] This is spelled out in more detail by Leonard Doohan in *Lay people and the Church*:[10]

Our present-day distinctions in the Church are neat and

clear-cut, especially in their canonical form, but such artificial distinctions are hardly faithful to the dynamic inter-
relationships between the community and its chosen
hierarchy in the first three centuries of the Church. With
the arrival of the emperor Constantine and his support
of the Church there developed a political community that
esteemed rank, and the Church soon mimicked this, estab-
lishing ranks for those who served the community. These
community leaders extended their control to the laity's
loss, eventually producing a two-tiered Church in which
even minor ministries were brought under the power of
the priesthood. Thus, we gradually pass from an ecclesiology of communion to an ecclesiology of power . . . The
passivity of laity increased in feudal times, and medieval
councils further consolidated it. Eventually, the Council
of Trent legitimized the separation between clergy and
people. Laity were then excluded from all active participation in the life of their Church, clerical control reaching
such proportions that in the minds of most people 'the
Church' came to mean the hierarchy.

The structure the Church inherited from the Middle Ages
still bears the marks of a feudal system: with archbishops,
bishops, clergy and laity mirroring the mediaeval secular
strata of princes, barons, knights and commoners.

We can therefore conclude that there was no distinction
between clergy and laity in the early Church, and that all
ministries and offices arose from within the local congregations. It must also be recognised, not only that difficulties
and factions were inherent in the Church from earliest times,
but that there were problems with church leaders right from
the start and that some of these difficulties sound remarkably
familiar to the Church today. Not only, for instance, is it
necessary for the writer of the first epistle of Peter to remind
the elders that they should be caring for their people rather
than behaving like earthly bosses (1 Pet. 5:3), but some
of the churches appear to be at the mercy of extremely
unsatisfactory leaders. A reading of Ephesians 4 should warn
us not to be over-romantic about the reliability of early

ministers: 'Then we shall no longer be children, or tossed one way and another, and carried hither and thither by every new gust of teaching, at the mercy of all the tricks people play and their unscrupulousness in deliberate deception'[9] (v. 14). What was going on in the Ephesian church? The writer is clearly concerned lest the faithful should be led astray by the very people who should be guiding them.

There are frequent references in the New Testament letters, particularly the pastoral letters, to the failings of leaders. When Paul sends Timothy to the Philippians he admits: 'There is nobody else that I can send who is like him and cares as sincerely for your well-being; they all want to work for themselves, not for Jesus Christ' (Phil. 2:21). In the following chapter, too, we read that there are church leaders whom Paul does not trust: 'Keep your eyes fixed on those who act according to the example you have from me. For there are so many people of whom I have often warned you, and now I warn you again with tears in my eyes, who behave like the enemies of Christ's cross' (Phil. 3:17–20). Warnings against false teachers become more common (2 Tim. 2:14–18; Jude and Titus); disagreements between church leaders and complaints against elders are accepted as commonplace (1 Tim. 5:17); and it seems to be necessary to emphasise that those chosen for church office should be reputable characters (1 Tim. 3:1–7).

It is clear, therefore, that there were difficulties in Christian ministry from the start. Since none of the models of leadership that arose in the Church were divinely ordained it should come as no surprise that the early days of this human institution should be as characterised by mistakes and squabbles as any other period. This does not mean that the Church should, or even could, have dispensed with the need for an ordained ministry, but just that we should try to sit lightly to all possible systems of Christian leadership, accepting them provisionally when they work to the good of the Church, and being prepared to dispense with them when they do not.

But above all we should bear in mind that the legacy of the first Christians is not one of hierarchy and division.

When Paul speaks in Romans 8 of the glorious freedom of being children of God, he does not suggest that this freedom is subject to intermediaries. Similarly, in Hebrews 10, the writer is addressing all Christians when he or she speaks of our right to enter the sanctuary – a right, incidentally, which is ours simply because Jesus Christ is our only high priest. It is stressed in Galatians that baptism confers on us all we need, and so wipes away all distinctions between people:

> Every one of you that has been baptised has been clothed in Christ. There can be neither Jew nor Greek, there can be neither slave nor freeman, there can be neither male nor female – for you are all one in Christ Jesus. And simply by being Christ's, you are that progeny of Abraham, the heirs named in the promise. (Gal. 3:27–9)

6

New Testament theology

The New Testament epistles reflect the immediate pastoral concerns of first century missionaries and teachers, and provide an invaluable record of the gradual evolution of church order. They also represent the forging of the earliest Christian theology, in which the writers explored the religious significance of the events that had changed their lives, and attempted an assimilation of some of the most ancient religious truths into the framework of the new revelations of God that had come through their experience of Jesus Christ.

For the first Jewish Christians, the confidence of being chosen by God was not one that could be challenged or diminished by the revelation of the person of God in Jesus Christ. As the Gospel came to be accepted by gentiles, however, the interpretation of being chosen (*eklektos*) necessarily widened to include all who were prepared to follow Christ. The gospels record Jesus using the term: for instance, at the end of his tale of the persistent widow, he reassures his listeners that God will 'see justice done to his elect' (Luke 18:8); and the privileged position of those whom God has chosen are mentioned in the eschatological warnings in Matthew 24 and Mark 13.

As this concept was incorporated into Christian thinking by the writers of the epistles, there is no hint of it being used to differentiate special leaders from the rest of the congregation. Rufus, one of the members of the congregation in Rome, is referred to as 'chosen servant' (Rom. 16:1); but it is more common for the term to be used in the plural to specify the members of the Christian community (2 Tim. 2:10; Tit. 1:1; 1 Pet. 1:1). As with the Old Testament understanding, the fact of being numbered among the chosen of God carried with it responsibility. Those of the diaspora to whom Peter writes in his first epistle, for instance, are chosen to be made holy and to obey and the moral imperative is spelled out even more clearly in Colossians: 'As the chosen of God, then, the holy people whom he loves, you are to be clothed in heartfelt compassion, in generosity and humility, gentleness and patience (3:12). *All* Christians are chosen; and while being thus chosen carries serious implications in terms of the life we should seek to lead, it does not carry with it any suggestion of leadership within the Church.

Two of the other concepts that were developed at this time, particularly in the more reflective epistles such as the the Letter to the Hebrews, encapsulate the New Testament teaching on priesthood. The first refers back to the Old Testament concept of *covenant* – so vital to Jewish belief and self-awareness – and creates the framework in which the Christian community is understood in terms of priesthood. The second relates to the identity of Christ. As the early Christian theologians considered the sacrificial nature of Jesus's life, death and resurrection, they recognised that one important sense in which it could be interpreted was in terms of priestly activity. The second interpretation of the concept of priesthood that is offered in the New Testament, therefore, is of *Jesus Christ as the great High Priest*. These, therefore, are the two uses of the word 'priest' that occur in the New Testament: the priesthood of all the faithful, and the priesthood of Christ.

Christ as the new covenant

We observed in chapter 2 how failure to live out the covenant relationship with God led the people of Israel first to formulate, and then to enslave themselves to, the Law. As the prophets attempted the difficult task of bringing people back into right relationship with God, they came to recognise that what was required was a new covenant; and in time the messianic hopes of the Jewish people began to cluster around this dream of a new covenant.

The Synoptic Gospels report Jesus as relating this hope to himself at the institution of the Eucharist (Matt. 26:28; Mark 14:24; Luke 22.20). Drawing on the ancient traditions, he describes a covenant that, like them, is sealed with blood: in this case through the shedding of his own blood in death; and he reinforces the association by making the shared cup of wine a symbol for his self-sacrifice. Early Christian writers were quick to pick up this thread, and the word 'covenant' occurs more than 30 times in the New Testament. As with the old covenant, the purpose of the new covenant is to bring people into right relationship with God.

Although the purpose of the new covenant mirrors the old, it builds on the lessons learned from past failure. There is a clear recognition that people enslaved to a Law cannot be in loving relationship with God, and Christians are therefore urged to be free from the Law: 'Christ set us free, so that we should remain free. Stand firm, then, and do not let yourselves be fastened again to the yoke of slavery' (Gal. 5:1).

The same writer compares the two covenants to show how the old one brought the Law while the new covenant brings freedom (4:21 ff). Again, in Romans, Paul stresses the faith aspect of covenant (ch. 4). But it is the writer of the Letter to the Hebrews who is most concerned to draw out the full significance of the new covenant signed and sealed in Christ's blood and who sets before the early Christian community the ideal of a covenant with God that can be understood as a way of life, rather than as religious observance or legalism. The only law that comes into force with the new covenant is the law that is written on people's hearts. This must lead both to greater freedom and to a deeper observance of the divine intention, since under this new law personal conscience can become the vehicle for the Holy Spirit.

We have seen that under the old covenant there arose a sacred caste of priests who took it upon themselves to become the intermediaries between God and the people.

Only these priests could visit the Holy Place, and no one was allowed to enter the Holy of Holies except for the high priest, who went in once a year (Heb. 9:6–7). The writer of Hebrews offers this priestly prerogative as a symbol for life under the new covenant. Whereas the system that grew up around the old covenant prevented people from relating to the deity, under the new covenant anyone can go into the sanctuary – or in other words anyone can exercise their priesthood – as long as

1. they have faith;
2. they have confessed their sins and accepted forgiveness; and
3. they are baptised:

> So as we go in, let us be sincere in heart and filled with faith, our hearts sprinkled and free from any trace of bad conscience, and our bodies washed with pure water. Let us keep firm in the hope we profess, because the one who made the promise is trustworthy. Let us be concerned for each other, to stir a response in love and good works. Do not absent yourselves from your own assemblies, as some do, but encourage each other; the more so as you see the Day drawing near. (Heb. 10:22–25)

Far from implying, as has sometimes been assumed, that the Epistle to the Hebrews relates to a doctrine of Christian priesthood, it would rather appear to suggest that as the old covenant led in time to the formation of an élite priesthood that cut the people off from the very relationship with God that the covenant had put on offer, the new covenant should inspire the Christian community to recognise that all Christians are called to exercise their priesthood.

This is born out when the writer encourages the people to grow up and stop behaving like children. There is no need for some to set themselves up as teachers since they should by now all be teachers; so the Hebrews are urged to accept their responsibility as mature members of the people of God, rather than being spoon fed. 'For though by this time you ought to be teachers, you need someone to teach you again the first principles of God's word' (5:12). As with the old covenant, the early Christians were finding it all too easy to abdicate responsibility and leave the business of priesthood to professionals. The later history of the Church was to show how real that danger was.

'Chosenness' and 'covenant' were two of the key concepts that New Testament Jewish writers took from their religious history and developed in their Christology. We have seen that in the Old Testament these concepts are inextricably linked, for the Israelites are chosen to enter into covenant relationship with God: 'So now, if you are really prepared to obey me and keep my covenant, you, out of all peoples, shall be my personal possession, for the whole world is mine. For me you shall be a kingdom of priests, a holy nation (Exod. 19:5–6). Right from the start, deep within the religious consciousness of the Jewish people, is the understanding that if they live in close and loving relationship with God, there is no need for intermediaries.

It is this theme that the writer of the First Letter of Peter takes up in encouraging the early Christians to take their common priesthood seriously, and that forms the basis of the doctrine of the priesthood of all believers. 'You are a chosen race, a royal priesthood, a consecrated nation, a people set apart to sing the praises of God who called you out of the darkness into his wonderful light' (2:9). It can, surely, be no coincidence that this mirrors so closely the passage from Deuteronomy in which the identity of God's chosen people is being established: 'For you are a people consecrated to Yahweh your God; of all the peoples on earth, you have been chosen by Yahweh your God to be his own people' (Deut. 7:6).

Both chosenness and covenant are inclusive terms in the Jewish Scriptures. If the covenant is for *all* the people, then responsible relationship with God is the privilege and duty of all. Similarly *the whole people* are chosen by God; and since they are chosen to be a nation of priests, there is no need or place for a professional religious class. St John the divine, writing to all the Christians in the seven churches of Asia, recognises that this privilege comes to the Christian by grace, through Jesus Christ, rather than because of desert or training; and in this way he identifies the process by which all the chosen become priests: 'Jesus Christ . . . loves us and has washed away our sins with his blood, and made us a Kingdom of Priests to serve his God and Father' (Rev. 1:6).

In the same way as the whole of the Jewish people entered into covenant with God, were called to be a 'nation of priests', so with the Christian community, membership of the priesthood of all believers does not imply individual priesthood, but corporate. The Spirit of Christ is at work in the world through the Christian community, so it is the whole community that exercises priesthood as the body of Christ.

Christians share in this priesthood by being part of the body of Christ on earth. But, as we have seen, Jesus did not come from the priestly tribe, and he could therefore be understood as a priest only by virtue of his priestly activity and nature, not his birth. The writer of the Letter to the Hebrews presents a case for the priesthood of Christ that would make sense to Jewish readers, by offering a prototype from their Scriptures. For it is to this epistle, written somewhere around AD 67, that we owe the model of priesthood based on the shadowy Old Testament figure of Melchizedek.[1]

Melchizedek

There are only two references to Melchizedek in the Old Testament: one in Genesis 14 which provides the primary text outlining the story, such as it is, of Melchizedek; the second in Psalm 110 where Melchizedek is first, and uniquely, recognised as prototype and forerunner, not of an order of priests, but of the Messiah. The references to Melchizedek in Hebrews suggest that the writer had access to other, poetic, literature that celebrated Melchizedek, but the source is unknown. Melchizedek is a Canaanite name meaning 'My King Is Righteousness', and he was a priest of God Most High, who in the Canaanite pantheon was the pagan god El 'Elyon'.

The short appearance of Melchizedek in the Old Testament narrative occurs when Abram has waged a battle against the Mesopotamian kings, to rescue his kinspeople; and has returned victorious bearing the plunders of war. The three verses concerning Melchizedek interrupt the narrative, coming between the arrival of the king of Sodom and his attempt to make a deal with Abram, which suggests that the incident might well be an interpolation.

> Melchizedek king of Salem brought bread and wine; he was a priest of God Most High. He pronounced this blessing:
> Blessed be Abram by God Most High,
> Creator of heaven and earth.
> And blessed be God Most High
> for putting your enemies into your clutches.
> And Abram gave him a tenth of everything. (Gen. 14:18–20)

While it is not obvious why this encounter should occur just here in the text, with no introduction or consequence, the story has a certain charm for Christians as the elements and actions of Melchizedek are evocative of Christian priesthood; and it is tempting to draw from it a concept of priesthood that is summed up in the eucharistic offering of bread and wine, the pronouncing of blessings and, of course, the claiming of tithes. Added to this is the fact that Melchizedek was a king, which has unfortunately sometimes been used to substantiate the kingly-priest tradition whereby priests constitute a holy élite, set apart from other believers.

From this basic story the author of Hebrews weaves a sophisticated theology that might well have helped members of the Jewish community to accept Jesus as Messiah. It is only in this letter that Christ is referred to as High Priest, a concept that would have held little attraction to converts from other traditions once Christianity started to gain ground in the Gentile world.

With such sparse material on which to base a theory, one might well ask why the author of the Epistle to the Hebrews introduced Melchizedek as a picture for Christ. In the light of the discovery of the Qumran Cave 11 Essene document amongst the Dead Sea Scrolls, it has been suggested that the letter was addressed to Zadokite priests who were the leaders of the Essene community at Qumran and who saw themselves as priests after the order of Melchizedek. Whether or not this is true, the letter appears to have been written for a Jewish Christian group that included a number of priest converts, and the author attempts to draw on their experience, particularly the offering of sacrifice at the altar, in creating a theology of Christ that interprets his death as a priestly offering of the one perfect sacrifice for all time.

Within the old order it was impossible to view Jesus Christ as a priest, since he came from the tribe of Judah. But Melchizedek, whose priesthood was based on promise, not birth, predates the division of Israel into tribes and so introduces the possibility of priests who were not born into the tribe of Levi.

So our Lord, of whom these things were said, belonged to a different tribe, the members of which have never done service at the altar; everyone knows he came from Judah, a tribe which Moses did not mention at all when dealing with priests. This becomes even more clearly evident if another priest, of the type of Melchizedek, arises who is a priest not in virtue of a law of physical descent, but in virtue of the power of an indestructible life. (Heb. 7:13–16)

As well as accounting for Christ's membership of a non-priestly tribe, in evolving this sacrificial theology the author also had to contend with the fact that for a number of early Christians, Jewish priests had been discredited. So on the one hand it was necessary to give Christ a priestly identity, but on the other to distance him from the less attractive elements of levitical history.

There were thus clear advantages in introducing a new order of priesthood, based on the figure of Melchizedek who offered bread and wine, blessed the great Abraham and was not only a king, but king of *Salem*, meaning peace, or as it was later known, Jerusalem. Not only was he unquestionably a priest without being a member of the tribe of Levi, but in receiving tithes from Abram of ten per cent of the booty and in blessing Abram, he assumes a superior status both to him and to his descendents, the sons of Levi. This allows the author to claim both that Jesus Christ is a priest and that his priesthood is of a higher order than that of Aaron and the whole line of levitical priests.

The Church has interpreted this to have implications for its own ordained ministry, and it is not uncommon to hear Christian priesthood described in terms of the order of Melchizedek. But although the Letter to the Hebrews has been taken as a prime text by those keen to support a sacerdotal view of Christian priesthood, Melchizedek is offered as a model of the priesthood of *Christ*, not of church officials; and an equally valid reading of the letter might actually suggest that since Christ is our high priest there is no longer any need for other priests.

Under the old Law a priest could enter the outer court of the Temple, but the inner court was restricted to the high priest, and even he could enter only once a year. In the same way, the writer explains, Jesus Christ is our high priest under the new Law, since he has passed through death into heaven. Priests under the old Law died and were replaced; but under the new Law there can be only one priest, because he lives for ever (vv. 23–4). Stretching the point a little, the writer compares this with Melchizedek for whom there is no birth or death date, which is taken to suggest that his priesthood, like that of Christ, is eternal rather than temporal. But if Christ's priesthood is proved by the fact of his resurrection, then all who share that resurrection must also share his priesthood.

The same qualities of sovereignty and eternal priesthood based on promise rather than birth had been identified by the psalmist in describing the necessary qualities of the coming Messiah in Psalm 110:

Yahweh will stretch out the sceptre of your power; from Zion you will rule your foes all around you. Royal dignity has been yours from the day of your birth, sacred honour from the womb, from the dawn of your youth. Yahweh has sworn an oath he will never retract, you are a priest for ever of the order of Melchizedek. (vv. 2–4)

The introduction of Melchizedek, the priest-king, which is so reminiscent of the Minoan civilisation of ancient Greece, is a theological construct adopted to suggest Melchizedek as a prototype for Christ. While elements of the gospel picture of the man Jesus suggest a non-kingly tradition, there are several strands for which a real or imagined royal lineage for Jesus is clearly important: for instance Matthew's birth narrative that traces his genealogy to David, and the symbolism surrounding the triumphal entry into Jerusalem on Psalm Sunday, recorded in all four gospels.

Even the genealogy, however, does not claim royal birth for Jesus, since to do that would necessitate claiming royalty for all the intervening males since David. It was not the man Jesus who was a king, any more than it was the man Jesus who was a priest: it is Christ who has passed through and beyond life into eternal majesty with God. Conversely, far from claiming that Christian priests have royal status, the text places Christ in a pre-eminent and unique position that obviates the necessity for priests in the Church.

The old order, under the Law, failed to bring perfection; but in the new order all are sanctified through Christ: 'This is the anchor our souls have, reaching right through inside the curtain where Jesus has entered as a forerunner on our behalf having become a high priest for ever, of the order of Melchizedek' (Heb. 6:20). The sacrifice of Christ has been offered once and for all, and does not need to be repeated (v. 27). It therefore makes the sacrifice of other priests unnecessary and whatever else Christian priests may be called to do, they do not, literally, offer sacrifice or attain atonement (10:11ff). Through Christ, the nature of priestly sacrifice itself is altered.

The unique sacrifice of Christ fulfils all the priestly sacrifices of atonement and makes them superfluous. But all believers in the new covenant have to make the sacrifices which were a part of the old covenant and which the prophets regarded as higher than all the material sacrifices prescribed by the law: prayer, praise, and thanksgiving, penitence, justice, kindness, love, the knowledge of God. The priesthood of the believers of the new covenant is expected to make spiritual sacrifices, sacrifices wrought by the Spirit.[2]

The writer is at pains to make it clear that Christian priesthood is not at all the same thing as Old Testament priesthood, but a new order – and this new order is referred to as the order of Melchizedech, to identify it with the model we see in Christ:

> Now if perfection had been reached through the levitical priesthood – and this was the basis of the Law given to the people – why was it necessary for a different kind of priest to arise, spoken of as being *of the order of Melchizedek* rather than of the order of Aaron? (Heb. 7:11ff)

The Epistle to the Hebrews (particularly chapter 5) presents a picture of the priest as one who offers gifts and sacrifices for sin, his own as well as others'. This means that a prime task of the priest, even Christ the great high priest, is to pray for others and to be gentle and sympathetic with the weak and wayward. Because Jesus Christ was tempted in all things, claims the author, he can sympathise with human weakness. Priesthood should therefore be associated with taking away the burden of sin, not with arousing guilt (Heb. 4:14–16). The history of the Christian Church has not always borne out this model of releasing people from the bondage of sin; on the contrary, the institutional Church has often appeared to be more intent on arousing than dispelling guilt.

So, far from furnishing us with a model for ordination, Melchizedek heralds in a new era in which there can be no such thing as a priestly élite. The order of Aaron was restricted, but the order of Melchizedek is open to all through Christ. In the same way as Melchizedek, without being a member of the priestly caste, is justified in performing priestly functions such as the giving of bread and wine and pronouncing of blessing, it can be argued that it is inappropriate for the Church to restrict such actions to a new caste of ordained priests rather than encouraging all the faithful to exercise their priesthood. As the author of the Epistle to the Hebrews claims Jesus Christ as our high priest according to this model, human priesthood becomes the prerogative of all; in other words, the priesthood of all believers.

7

History and Reformation

By tracing the history of the idea of covenant, first through the Old Testament Scriptures and then as the idea was developed by early Christian writers, we have seen a close parallel between the relationship agreed between God and the Israelites as the chosen race, and the fresh start that the writers of the New Testament felt that they had been offered through the life, death and resurrection of Jesus Christ.

It is something of an irony that after the destruction of the Temple the Jews can be seen to have gradually moved away from clericalised temple worship and to base their sacramental life in the home and community. At the same time, the Christian Church began to take the sacraments away from ordinary people and to imprison them within the Church. So it is that the Christian Mass bears similarities to earlier Jewish cultic rituals, while the Jewish sabbath evening meal resembles far more closely the reality of the Last Supper.

Over the centuries the people of Israel had allowed a priestly caste to arise, which, although it was meant to mediate between God and humanity, in effect separated people from God. Part of the excitement of the New Testament is the renewed perception that all are called to be in this special relationship with God. So, although various patterns of leadership emerged in the New Testament churches, nothing approaching a clericalised institution came into existence until much later.

As we move further from the events of the life of Jesus Christ and the growth of the first Christian communities, the more the Church comes to resemble any other human institution. The pressing question therefore becomes: how long did it take for the cycle to repeat itself, and for the Church to move from being a community of priests to being the stage on which a small number of the elect could take office and enter on a career structure?

The first reference to clergy as opposed to laity occurs in Clement of Rome's Epistle to the Corinthians probably written in around AD 95. He still uses 'bishop' and 'presbyter' interchangeably (4ff), but he is the first Christian writer to demote the *laos* to an inferior position in the Church; and he does this, significantly and perhaps ominously, by reference to the levitical priesthood:

> The High Priest . . . has his own proper station assigned to him, the priesthood has its own station, there are particular ministries laid down for the Levites, and the layman is bound by regulations affecting the laity.(40)

Clement is not an altogether reliable historian. There is no evidence that the Church at the turn of the century had any office that resembled that of high priest or Levite, any more than the Arabian phoenix, described elsewhere in the same letter, could have been studied by an ornithologist. In this letter he was trying to persuade the rather headstrong people of Corinth not to sack their bishops:

> we cannot think it right for these men now to be ejected from their ministry, when, after being commissioned by the Apostles (or by other reputable persons at a later date) with the full consent of the Church, they have since been serving Christ's flock in a humble, peaceable and disinterested way, and earning everybody's approval over so long a period of time. It will undoubtedly be no light offence on our part, if we take their bishopric away from men who have been performing its duties with this impeccable devotion.(44)

In other words, the distinction between priest and laity was introduced by a bishop to protect his clergy from the people. It had nothing to do with encouraging Christians to greater efforts in ministry, or offering to serve the community more self-sacrificially. It was simply introduced as a device to protect the clergy from those who would like to dismiss them. This was a moment when a cold shiver should have run down the spine of the Church and warned of abuses to come.

Apart from Clement, it is not until the third century that the distinction between clergy and laity is widely observed, although the fact that several writers found it necessary to emphasise the priestly nature of the whole Christian community suggests that it was gradually becoming an issue. Both Justin and Irenaeus in the second century refer to all Christians as being priests, and later the same assumption is made by Clement of Alexandria and Origen.[1] Tertullian (c 160–240) refers to the priesthood of all believers in several of his works, and although it is common to pay scant regard to his later works, written under the influence of Montanism, this does not alter the fact that there were still many Christians who assumed that the priesthood of the faithful *meant* the priesthood.

> Are not we laymen priests also? It is written: 'He hath also made us a kingdom and priests to God and his Father.' . . . If you have the rights of a priest in your own person when necessity arises, you ought likewise to have the discipline of a priest, where it is necessary to exercise his rights.[2]

Tertullian drew out the implication that if all Christians are priests, then all can when necessary perform such priestly functions as exorcism, baptism and eucharistic celebration:

> But where no college of ministers has been appointed, you, the laity, must celebrate the eucharist and baptize; in that case you are your own priests, for where two or three are gathered together, there is the church, even if these three are lay people.[3]

In *De Fuga in Persecutione*[4] he specifies that in such an emergency any three Christians can celebrate the Eucharist. However, he clearly did not consider such practices to be acceptable in normal circumstances, for he himself criticised

the Montanists for allowing lay people to celebrate the
Eucharist when there was no real need.

It was still normal for those who emerged as the natural
leaders of the community to be invited to celebrate at the
Eucharist, so that in a sense every Eucharist was a celebration by the whole community.

Apostolic succession

The emergence of a quasi-magical process by which something special was handed (literally) from Christ to the first
disciples and from them to other favoured persons who were
then the only ones to truly count as priests does not appear
to have arisen in the first few centuries of the Christian
Church. It is true that the apostolicity of the Church is
considered vital, but it is clear that for these writers it is the
Church that is apostolic, not the succession.

It is important not to confuse the apostolic succession with
the laying on of hands at ordination. The priestly formation
should be understood as the calling and commissioning by
the Christian community, of which the laying on of hands
becomes a symbol. The Church frequently falls into this
trap of confusing sacraments with facts, thereby diminishing
the sacramental grace.

The whole point of a sacrament is that it is *not* the thing
itself but a very special sign of it. For instance, it would be
ridiculous to claim that a man and a woman fall in love at
their marriage ceremony, or that a baptised person suddenly
stops sinning and begins to live in a new way on entering
the baptismal water. Similarly a priest does not suddenly
become true to the apostolic teaching just because someone
has laid (special) hands on her or him. Rather, the ordination
ceremony is the gathering up of that person's whole religious
understanding and significance into one symbolic action.
When we come to explore the nature of the sacraments in
chapter 9, we shall find that they have nothing to do with
magic, but that they symbolise and signify. It is also import-

ant to recognise their role in empowering people, which does not depend on disempowering others.

According to the Acts of the Apostles, the first apostles laid hands on those whom they converted and this action was generally associated with a pentecostal experience in which the new Christian received the Holy Spirit. The action was certainly not reserved for religious leaders, but was a sacrament offered to the new convert, sometimes at the same time as baptism. In most of the mainstream churches this sacrament is still available to all the faithful at confirmation.

In view of this catholicity, it is somewhat surprising that the Church should later have become exclusive about the laying on of hands at ordination. If there *is* an unbroken line of such gestures going back to the person of Christ, which is far from certain, then everyone who has received the laying on of hands at confirmation is part of this apostolic succession. But given that we hold to the apostolic teaching, it hardly matters whether or not this line of succession is unbroken or not. We should be trying to extend the sacrament to as many people as possible, rather than tightening up controls to keep out any whom we consider should not be included.

Patristic period

The first clear reference to the three-fold ministry comes at the dawn of the second century, in Ignatius's Epistle to the Philadelphians, when he writes: 'there is but one bishop, with his clergy and my own fellow-servitors the deacons'. The words 'bishop' and 'presbyter' continued to be used interchangeably until into the second century, to refer to local officers in the churches. As the apostles died out, these officers began to take over their work and gradually came to form the recognised body of church leaders.

Cyprian, who was bishop of Carthage from 248 to 258 was largely responsible for sacerdotalising the Christian ministry by comparing it to the Old Testament priesthood and referring to the Eucharist in terms of an Old Testament sacrifice. He was also the first to say that the priest presides at the Eucharist in the place of Christ.[5]

As this understanding of priesthood gradually took root during the patristic period it was perhaps inevitable that the Church should become more hierarchical and exclusive, until in the fifth century Jerome was able to insist that there could be no Church without priests.[6]

Nevertheless, even when the subject of priesthood was addressed at the Council of Chalcedon in 451, there was still no question of priests being chosen and appointed other than by the whole community (Canon 6). It was many more centuries before the Church introduced the possibility of absolute ordinations;[7] and even as late as the end of the eleventh century Guerricus of Igny could write: 'The priest does not consecrate by himself, he does not offer himself, but the whole assembly of believers consecrates and offers along with him'.[8]

What we find if we look at the model of the early Church, therefore, is not an hierarchical structure operating within a closed shop, but a democratic, functional body of people, responding to the changing needs and opportunities of the moment. Why did this change?

One reason for the development of a clearer and more controlled structure was undoubtedly the simple need for efficiency in evangelising and then assimilating people from vastly different backgrounds into the Church. With the prime commission of handing on the apostolic teaching, it was necessary to ensure that there was a consensus of opinion as to what that teaching was and how it related to the various changing circumstances. Related to this was the operation of the Church in regard to new interpretations of doctrine, and the differentiation of orthodoxy from heresy. To control the output of official doctrine and faith, it was helpful to have a body of people whose guidance was accepted as being representative of the Church. It should always be remembered, however, that the people who pro-pounded the ideas and interpretations that came to be con-demned as heretical, were not rogues out to destroy Christian teaching, but devout Christians, many of them bishops or missionaries, who cared deeply about the Church and sincerely believed that what they were teaching was orthodox.

As well as ensuring continuity and orthodoxy, the development of a clerical class also reflects two less desirable realities. The first is the existence in the Church, as anywhere else, of human ambition and the desire for privilege. It would be good to be able to claim that these did not raise their ugly heads in the early Church, but given that they have been much in evidence in the Church in later centuries, there is no reason to believe that the early Church escaped them altogether. The seductions of spiritual superiority, of the control of the inner lives of the faithful, of the belief that by joining an élite one can ensure that God is on one's side, is responsible for much of the damage done to and by the Church over the centuries.

But it is also difficult to escape the conclusion that male chauvinism too, as so often in Church history, played its part in the growth of a professional clerical class, and on occasions the development of hierarchy appears to coincide rather obviously with the putting down of prominent women. So, for example, Hippolytus rails against a community that accords respect to two women who were presumably engaged in excellent work in their church:

> They have been deceived by two females, Priscilla and Maximilla by name, whom they hold to be prophetesses, asserting that into them the Paraclete spirit entered . . . They magnify these females above the Apostles and every gift of Grace, so that some of them go so far as to say that there is in them something more than Christ. These people agree with the Church in acknowledging the Father of the universe to be God and Creator of all things, and they also acknowledge all that the Gospel testifies of Christ. But they introduce novelties in the form of fasts and feasts, abstinences and diets of radishes, giving these females as their authority.[9]

Fear of the female sex is only thinly veiled in this outburst, and the reduction of the women's life of self-discipline and abstinence to 'diets of radishes' curiously demeaning.

A Church that had turned away from the apostolic witness of the early women disciples and which apparently omitted women's writings from the canon of Scripture, was unlikely to take great delight in the leadership of women in the Church. If the Holy Spirit chose, as did Jesus, to call women to the work of Christian ministry, then the only way to ensure that men could retain pre-eminence in this area was to create an ordained priesthood into which women were refused entry. In this way a group was formed which had clearly-defined boundaries, and it was not long before this group assumed power and control in the Church.

Need for reform

By the Middle Ages this group had achieved a virtual monopoly of land, wealth, education and culture. Bishops were princes, monasteries were the forerunners of universities and the Church was one of the strongest landowners in most European countries. The institution bore little resemblance to the community of Christians of the first century, and increasingly over the next few centuries the voices of lone Christians are raised in protest.

Hildegard of Bingen, for instance, a woman who did enjoy some measure of respect, though she was frequently distrusted and diminished by the clergy, wrote:

> God and Justice will say in turn: 'How long will we suffer and endure these ravening wolves, who ought to be physicians and are not?' But because they have the power of preaching, imposing penance and granting absolution, for that reason they hold us in their grasp like ferocious beasts. Their crimes fall upon us and through them the whole Church withers, because they do not proclaim what is just; and they destroy the law like wolves devouring sheep. They are voracious in their drunkenness and they commit copious adulteries, and because of such sins they judge

us without mercy. For they are also plunderers of their congregations, through their avarice, devouring whatever they can; and with their offices they reduce us to poverty and indigence, contaminating both themselves and us. For this reason let us judge and single them out in a fair trial, because they lead us astray rather than teaching us what is right.[10]

The same theme can be seen in visual form in some of the art of the period. For instance, in Hexham Abbey in Northumberland there is a stone carving of preacher and congregation in which the preacher appears as a wolf leering down at the upturned faces of the foolish geese he is about to devour. This sharp and graphic indictment of both clergy and laity, rings as true today as in the fifteenth century.

If we turn to the religious orders, we find that neither Benedict nor Francis was ordained. At some later period their Orders came to be dominated by clergy, but they were essentially lay at their foundation. Francis and his friars turned from the pomp of the Church and attempted to live out the simplicity and poverty of the Gospel; Bernard of Clairvaux dreamt of a return to the purity of the early Church, when the apostles fished for souls rather than gold; and most of the mediaeval reform movements such as the Lollards and Waldenses sought to wean the Church away from idolatry, to a more simple way of life and worship.

The long struggle to reinstate the laity as the people of God took different forms and was undertaken through varying means. It is clear from reading history that the church hierarchies were threatened by the possible empowerment of the laity, which is why the battles to make the Bible and liturgies available in the vernacular were so long and bloody. William Tyndale, who encountered struggle, persecution and finally martyrdom in the cause of translating the Bible into English, knew perfectly well that what he was attempting was subversive and that reading the Scriptures for themselves was likely to endow the laity with a new independence and understanding which would diminish their dependence on the clergy.

But the greatest revolt against the clericalisation of the Church came with the Reformation. The trickles of doubt began to flow into a steady stream of discontent which gathered force until it burst upon the religious consciousness and life of Europe. Perhaps it was the sharp wit of Erasmus at the beginning of the sixteenth century which drew the first blood, with such anti-clerical remarks as his claim that to call a layman a cleric, priest or monk was to insult him unpardonably.

In the following years the Reformation swept across the continent, borne along by men such as Luther, Calvin, Wyclif and Zwingli. Luther, in particular, criticised the clergy for their frequent failure to represent Christ; and he used to devastating effect the etymology of the word 'vicar', which means 'in place of':

> See how different Christ is from his successors, although they all would wish to be his vicars. I fear that most of them have been too literally his vicars. A man is a vicar only when his superior is absent. If the pope rules, while Christ is absent and does not dwell in his heart, what else is he but a vicar of Christ? What is the church under such a vicar but a mass of people without Christ? Indeed, what is such a vicar but an antichrist and an idol? How much more properly did the apostles call themselves servants of the present Christ and not vicars of an absent Christ.[11]

Martin Luther was also one of the main proponents of the doctrine of the priesthood of all believers, which is why at least until this century the phrase would have been anathema to many a Roman Catholic. But the Roman Catholic Church now has as much to contribute to the debate as to how all Christians are to exercise their priesthood as have any of the reformed churches.

> There is no true, basic difference between laymen and priests, princes and bishops, between religious and secular, except for the sake of office and work, but not for the sake of status. They are all of the spiritual estate, all are truly priests, bishops and popes. But they do not all have

the same work too. Just as all priests and monks do not have the same work.[12]

Once the Reformation had started it was unlikely to cease, and throughout the following centuries we see a progression of reformers and new movements that turned away from the excesses and faults of those who went before: Anabaptists, Mennonites, Presbyterians, Quakers, Baptists, Methodists. Through the successes and failures of these movements, protest, reform and non-conformity became an established part of Christian history.

The wheel turns

If we look at these new and recurring movements in the light of our study of priesthood, two salutory truths emerge. First, although many of them propounded sensible and worthy doctrines and called people back to the fundamentals of the faith, some of them suffered badly from the excesses of their lunatic fringes. Reforming zeal, which in the rational, sensitive and educated can spawn sound religious sub-cultures, when it takes root in less cultivated soil can grow rank weeds of idiocy at an alarming rate. The growth of cults in the twentieth century should warn us that a Church that allowed a free-for-all in organising worship and deter-mining doctrine would be prey to every excess that the religious imagination can foster. One of the important func-tions of the Church, and in particular of those who exercise leadership in the Church, is and always has been to forge an orthodoxy that adequately reflects both the original Gospel and the understanding of all Christian people. This, as we have observed, is the true meaning of the apostolic suc-cession.

The other uncomfortable truth that confronts us as we look at the history of religious reform, is that however charis-matic and dramatic the initial changes, and however impress-ive the lives of the first adherents of that reform, it is not unusual for this ardour to become dulled, and for the refor-

med movement to suffer many of the same faults and difficulties as the organisation against which it first reacted.
This can be seen particularly clearly in the case of church
leadership, where in most of the Reformed, Protestant and
Nonconformist churches, the role of the ordained minister
is just as powerful and potentially corrupt as in the older
church traditions from which they split. The very position
of the pulpit from which the minister preaches in some
Scottish Presbyterian churches illustrates this point in
graphic form.

These two unpalatable truths should warn against any
simplistic desire to initiate new church movements. True
reform must mean reform of what exists, not the creation of
different permutations, and several of the reformers were
well aware of this. One of the tragedies of English church
history is that John Wesley, who longed for the Church of
England to be true to its best traditions, was eased out of the
Anglican Church; and his followers, who should have been
setting an example of how to be good Anglicans, were hived
off into what became the Methodist Church. True reform is
rare, which is why Christians of all denominations were so
excited at the advances made by the Second Vatican Council
in our own century, and why there is such general dismay
now that much of that genuine reform appears to be under
threat.

The need for order or *taxis* has been part of the understanding of the Christian Church as a community since the
very first days. What Paul, Peter, Apollos and others were
arguing over, beneath the philosophical interpretations of
the gospel, were practical matters relating to what was
acceptable for followers of Jesus Christ. Christianity is not
an individualistic religion, it is a community movement, a
common priesthood of believers; and it matters what is
expounded and believed within that common priesthood.
One of the defences of an ordained ministry, therefore, is
that it can perform the function of final arbiter of what
is consonant with Christian teaching and what should be
condemned as heresy.

The trouble with this defence, however, is that the only

way to define heresy is as that which the Church does not accept as orthodox. Plenty of actions and institutions within the Church would appear to be contrary to the vision of Christ, including, perhaps, the formation of an ordained priesthood itself; while calls to return to a purer and more literal approach to the Gospel have invariably been condemned as heretical by the institutional Church.

One of the religious truths that has been revealed in Scripture is that human beings are created and called to be in partnership with God, and that this call, this vocation, is for all. The ancient Israelites perceived this truth, but gradually lost it as they built a structure to preserve their religious purity. The early Church rediscovered it, then as Christianity grew and flourished the first flush of enthusiasm abated, the ideal was lost and the same cycle began again. Reform movements sprang up all over Europe, recalling people to the original purity of vision, condemning the corruption and power of the clergy, the disablement of the laity, the abuse of faith and sacrament; and again the wheel turned, with the new becoming worn, the ideal becoming pragmatic and the need for reform recurring again and again. Observing such an oft-repeated cycle it is difficult for any Christian to resist cynicism and despair.

But the message cannot be ignored. Its imprint is deep on the pages of the Bible, its implications startlingly alive in every craving for true religion, every attempt at reform. Humanity is called by God to exercise priesthood in the world, and this is too important a mission to be left to the few. Even if the whole of the Bible and history is about the priesthood of all believers and humanity's failure to live it out, that does not let us off the hook. We must ask why we have so consistently failed and how the structures must be changed for reform to be true.

Human ambition and the lust for power and prestige undoubtedly play their part on occasions. As the fervour of the original reformers dies out and a new class of professionals assume privilege in their own right, the *enfant terrible* becomes a big fish in a new, albeit smaller pool, and begins to succumb to the same temptations in a different form. But another factor, that operates just as fatally, is the drift towards apathy by lay people, who find that while they may be fired with enthusiasm for a time, it is difficult to maintain the first fresh vigour while conducting the normal affairs of life year in and year out. It is so much easier to pay someone else to do the job, and leave them to it.

Reformation and the sacraments

Before we leave the sad story of the cyclical nature of church reform, there is another recurring feature that cannot be ignored, and that is the way in which the reform movements so often allowed themselves to be deprived of the more sacramental aspects of Christianity.

At one level this is not at all surprising, for the sacramental activity of the Church is the arena in which clergy power has been most absolute. Therefore, as the reformers turned away from the forms of worship over which the clergy had control, they necessarily allowed themselves to be ousted from the sacraments of the Church. Each reform movement gradually, for instance, lost the centrality of the Eucharist, which allowed the unreformed Church to keep that sacrament, hedging it in yet further with clerical legalism. So one of the most effective ways in which the Church has traditionally dealt with reform is to grow a new skin over the sacraments, leaving the new movements impoverished in sacramental theology and practice.

There are exceptions to this rule, as for example with the Baptist Church which, far from losing the sacrament of baptism has claimed it and journeyed with it. This would suggest that there is no intrinsic reason why reforming churches should not lay claim to the centrality of eucharistic celebration.

This oft-repeated cycle of reform and reaction will no doubt continue to operate in our own time, though we may be moving into an era in which reform can be accommodated within orthodoxy rather than creating schism. If this happens, then genuine reform, working from within the institution rather than being excluded from it, might become a realistic possibility for the first time since the early days of Christianity.

To be effective, reform should be radical in theology, determined to look for the truth whatever has become the norm through habit. It should have a strong doctrine and practice of those sacraments that are important to the Christian life, and it should be rooted in the best of history and tradition. Perhaps above all, it should be prepared to examine ways in which the Church, despite having gone sadly astray so many times, might begin to understand and obey the divine command that we should be a priestly people.

The impact of ordination on the Church now

If our failure to understand the nature of religious truth has become so deeply entrenched that we cannot learn the lessons of the Old Testament, the early Church or the Reformation, is there any hope for the Church or for a world that is crying out for hope and meaning? Why have the different attempts at reform not produced a Church that mirrors the passion and humility of Jesus Christ and that can support people in their attempts to live Christ-like lives in the world?

We saw in earlier chapters that the present system of ordained priesthood is not the only possible model. It was a fairly late development, and coexisted for many years with alternative systems and structures. Over the centuries, the Church has adopted a complex hierarchical system that is phenomenal in terms of its organisation and catholicity and has much to commend it as a factor in the growth of the Church as a bureaucratic institution; but this model is not sacrosanct and should be viewed as no more than provisional.

There is, and always has been, work to be done in the Church and by the Church in the world. It is right and proper for the Church to commission, and in many cases to pay, able and qualified people to do these tasks. But that does not mean that these people must be ordained as priests. If priesthood is nothing but a certain sort of employment by the Church, then there is no sense in which it is sacramental. To participate in the sacrament of priesthood is something quite different from being paid by the Church to do a job.

The fact that our present understanding and practice of ordained priesthood is unbiblical and – at least up until the fourth century – untraditional, however, does not make it any easier to see how the Church would have developed and spread so effectively without such a professional group. The stamp of approval of orthodoxy may on occasions appear to have had more to do with power and expediency than with the guidance of the Holy Spirit; nevertheless, the succession of professional clergy, handing down a received body of belief from one generation to the next, has provided a point of reference against which new exploration and revelation can be tested.

This class of Christians has also kept faith alive and been responsible for evangelism and the spiritual care of the faithful throughout ages when there was little popular religious enthusiasm. If there had been no ordained priesthood at these times, with the express charge of purveying the Christian Gospel, it is by no means certain that traditions would have been handed down or necessary tasks performed. Yet there is no doubt that there is, at the end of the twentieth century, a widening gap between the faithful and the institution. This was recognized by Leonard Doohan in his article in *The Way*:

> The relationship between laity and hierarchy continues to be the fundamental problem in the Church . . . The rift between the two parts of the Church continues to grow as increasing numbers of the faithful see the hierarchy and its values as unimportant to their lives. Some move from one christian tradition to another, many do not attend Church as frequently as they used to, others do not take the hierarchy's teaching authority seriously.[1]

It is not uncommon for deeply committed Christians to find themselves in conflict with their clergy; and although there is nothing very new or unusual about this, the fact that many lay people are now at least as highly educated and powerful as their clergy, often as well-versed in theology and more involved in educating or caring for people, can add to the bitterness of the rift. Lay people can be deeply distressed to discover clergy who believe they have rights of ownership over the Church and who are quick to suggest that anyone who disagrees with them should move out as quickly as possible.

Conversely clergy, who are uncomfortable at being less respected and more openly challenged and who can feel embattled by their association with a shrinking institution, frequently lose their nerve as their work achieves no noticeable results, and they are confronted with a deep crisis of confidence over what it means to be an ordained priest. In the face of questioning from within and an increasing sense of irrelevance without, faith can take an uncomfortable battering and the human costs can be high. So, before going on to examine how we might develop a more sacramental and efficient understanding of priesthood, we shall look at the effects of the present system on the clergy themselves and on the laity.

Clergy

One of the most difficult tensions with which ordained priests have to live is the question of whether their priesthood should be understood as a vocation or a profession. In most cases they will have started on the path to ordination because of a belief that they were called to serve God sacrificially, putting the mission of Jesus at the centre of their lives and devoting as much of their time, energy, money and relationships to God as possible.

They then undertook a period of training which, depending on their own personality and the ethos of the institution they attended, may either have instilled in them a deep belief in their own superiority or shaken the foundations of their faith. Thrown into the apprenticeship of a curacy some will have had their enthusiasm and ideals squeezed out by an older priest, as well as picking up a number of bad ecclesiastic habits and cynicisms on the way. Finally they arrive in their first parish, determined that this church at least will bear the imprint of their personality and ministry. Although this is an extreme picture, elements of it are by no means uncommon.

After ordination many fall into the habit(!) of adopting clerical dress and accept as inevitable the drabness of a uniform that can give men an uncanny resemblance to undertakers and women the unmistakable air of super-numerary Girl Guides. The clerical collar, still resisted far too rarely, becomes a badge of office and, although it has been associated with ordination only for the last 100 years and has nothing to do with priestly functions, it somehow becomes imbued with religious significance. Sometimes clerical dress is excused on the basis that it acts as a badge by which all may know that this person is available to them in a priestly capacity should they need it; but it is questionable whether clergy have any higher propensity than others to strike up deep and meaningful conversations with those they meet in the course of their daily lives.

In churches where celibacy is not the norm, a number of these young priests marry and soon encounter the normal conflicts between work and family life. The initial longing that all their time, talents and material goods should be offered to God has to wrestle with the reality of shortage of money, lack of private time and various forms of attention-seeking by nearest and dearest human beings who consider that they have at least as much right to love and attention as the poor of the parish. Concepts such as 'my day off', 'holidays', 'proper remuneration', 'expenses' and 'decent salary' take the place of the former ideals of sacrifice and self-giving, and the possibilities of promotion within what comes to be perceived as a career structure begin to look enticing.

Many priests would be hard put to say whether they do, in fact, see their work as a profession or a vocation. It probably would not matter very much which understanding they opted for, as the Church could benefit from either: a professional group of workers with clear and achievable objectives, or people who are willing to sacrifice everything in working for the good of others. But uncertainty over which camp they are meant to be in leads many clergy into confusion, and results in either guilt at their own inadequacies or resentment over the demands made on them by others.

Ordination can prove deeply damaging to the personal relationships of the clergy. Leaving aside the question that arises in some denominations of the effect of enforced celibacy on healthy human beings, the system that has given clergy inflated status within the Church has also tended to rob them of deep and meaningful human relationships. There is nothing very revolutionary about recognising that it can be difficult for clergy to make or maintain close friendships and that as a group they are amongst the loneliest people in our society.

A fair proportion of a Christian's time and energy is expended within the ambit of the local church, and that is the pool within which many Christians are most likely to share interests and experiences with like-minded people. Yet clergy are often fearful of getting close to members of their congregations: partly lest this be seen as unprofessional favouritism, and partly because it makes them vulnerable to all the usual dangers of attraction, misunderstanding and betrayal that arise in personal relationships. While for some this represents simply a slight insecurity about role or a lack of confidence stemming from natural shyness, in others it follows from a more formalised recommendation during training that personal relationships within one's congregation should be eschewed as far as possible.

Such a policy is so clearly dangerous in terms of personal development and support for public work that it is difficult to believe it could still be current. However, it is not uncommon for the correspondence pages of the religious press to air the debate even today, and the rousing pronouncements of those who insist that friendship within the congregation in which one ministers is inappropriate, make it all too clear why so many clergy are friendless.

The social isolation of clergy is well-attested to in the annals of fiction where, from Jane Austen's stuffy young curates or Trollope's self-satisfied cathedral chapters to Susan Howatch's sexually-disoriented middle-aged clerics, the ordained appear as a class slightly apart from the rest of society: gauche with the opposite sex even when married to them, ill at ease in informal gatherings away from the womb of the Church and frequently deriving their sole pleasure from what others would consider lonely and melancholy pursuits and obsessions. While for every such fictional stereotype most of us could name two normal well-adjusted clergy friends, the frequency with which this tortured gentleman recurs in literature suggests that his existence is recognised by a large proportion of the reading population.

Related, perhaps, to the difficulties such clergy have in forming and sustaining personal relationships is the effect that living as an ordained person can have on personal morality. History groans with the tales of evil done in the name of the Church: torture in the Inquisition and murder in the Crusades, the greed of wealthy abbots and bishops, the intrigues of popes and cardinals. But it is just as spiritually dangerous to be a 'professional Christian' now. It is so easy to think that normal rules of behaviour do not quite apply, that there are special circumstances which make a slight but significant difference to moral judgements if one is working in an official capacity for God. This temptation to adopt a superior attitude to morality is bound to be deeply damaging to those who fall under its spell.

Clergy sometimes complain that the world expects them to be paragons of virtue, valiantly upholding a level of morality that is unattainable by others. It is, of course, true that people can foster unrealistic expectations of their clergy, as they can of mothers, accountants, teachers or anyone else; and no one is likely to bear the weight of the role of super-Christian for very long without cracking. But what angers many lay people and brings the Church into disrepute is not that clergy have feet of clay, but that they sometimes fail to meet the basic standards of morality and decency that are expected of other ordinary members of society.

Secular newspapers are quick to capitalise on the more public disgraces of clergy, to the embarrassment of ordained and lay alike; but there are other less exciting – though no less alarming – examples of clerical misdemeanour, that eat into the soul of the Church. It does not matter whether what is at issue is the exploitation of generosity for personal gain, illicit and unprofessional sexual relationships, or the uncharitable squabbles and inability to forgive that have been known to afflict some cathedral chapters and parishes. In each case the question remains: is this behaviour consonant with ordinary Christian morality? It is particularly important to ask such questions when clergy are placed in situations where they are not adequately supervised or even, in some cases, held accountable.

Matthew records Jesus advising his followers that claims to be his followers must be backed up by tangible benefits in terms of life style: 'By their fruits ye shall know them' (7:15-16). Using the same image but in a different context, he tells the story of the wicked tenants and warns that the kingdom of God will be taken from them and given to the people who produce the fruit (21:43). The chief priests and scribes have the wit to recognise immediately that he is referring to them, and they react with anger.

It is just as apposite now, in our own church situations, to say of the ordained clergy that we shall know them by their fruits. Do they reflect anything of the love of God in their personal relationships, their families, their marriages? Do their financial or business deals bear scrutiny? What can be said of the moral and spiritual life of the congregations committed to their care?

As well as the ordinary temptations to which we are all subject, we expect our clergy to grapple with the seductions of power. Within the present system it is quite reasonable that clergy should be put in positions of authority, but that authority can be abused when it is confused with power: whether it is power to organise worship, to dominate the parochial decision-making processes, to keep denominations apart or to give absolution and administer the body and blood of Christ. Maggie Ross, in *Pillars of Flame*, courageously confronted the reality of this hunger for power at the heart of Christian eucharistic worship:

> In today's churches, at least at the official level, envy continues to reserve the eucharistic prayer as the exclusive right of members of the clerical club. This may be a harsh and unpalatable reality, but it is time we faced it before

the worship of self-seeking power destroys not only Christianity, which is the worship of self-emptying love (and therefore self-restrained power), but also the whole earth. Exploring these truths with naked honesty, even ruthlessness, will release us into Christ's freedom and is a new hope for the future.[2]

On top of all this, the professionalising of faith can, though obviously it need not and often does not, lead to impoverishment of a priest's own spiritual life. To bear responsibility for the instigation and conduct not only of one's own, but of a whole community's prayer life, for week after week and year after year, can dull the edge of the sharpest enthusiasm, particularly when every creative innovation has been tried and no one else offers a fresh perspective. The excitement of the lay person who has to organise life rather carefully to get to extra services is not easily matched when it is a duty to attend; for choice is always sweet, even in the case of liturgy.

Faced with such a catalogue of pitfalls and dangers that can beset the ordained priest, it is all the more remarkable that so many ordained clergy live out godly and ordered lives, relating in love to those around them, regular in prayer and devotion and resistant to the subtle and ever-changing wiles of the devil. It should also be noted that other professional and semi-professional groups within the Church face their own range of temptations and difficulties: choir members, servers, bell-ringers, chalice bearers and pastoral assistants all know that to be on duty can subtly change the nature of both worship and relationships.

The clerical identity crisis

Over and above all these difficulties that ordained priests have to face is the fundamental existential doubt that can eat away at their sense of purpose and self-esteem. For as secular professions have taken over the majority of the roles that used to be the preserve of clergy, so it has become increasingly difficult to define what a priest is. This is all to the good, because while priests were responsible for teaching, counselling and the organisation of charitable work no one asked the most important question of what ordination is for.

A. A. K. Graham, writing in *Theology* in 1968, pointed to the diminishing role of the clergy: 'the clergy no longer figure prominently in the magistracy, no longer largely control primary education, no longer are responsible for poor-relief, nor do the Church's views on moral matters carry the weight that they once did.'[3] He went on to argue that ordained ministry is still needed, but for positive reasons of displaying, enabling and involving, not for negative reasons of covering the jobs that no one else happens to be doing. We have had to learn to avoid a God-of-the-gaps theology: we must now have the confidence to eschew a priesthood-of-the-gaps philosophy.

The increased expertise and involvement of the laity in the churches has helped to move us towards a position in which lay people are beginning to exercise their priesthood in the world; but it has thrown into sharper relief the uncertainties over what functions can be performed only by those who are ordained. Lay people are involved and successful in all spheres of religious life: lay theologians are instrumental in carving out a developing theology, able lay preachers are in great demand for sharing their vision for the Church, worship can be planned and executed with as much dignity and honour by lay people as ordained priests, most churches would benefit from having a lay administrator, secular charities feed the hungry and visit the orphans and widows, counsellors and support groups replace the priestly confessor. What is left that can be done exclusively by the ordained person, that will justify their years of training, the importance they attach to their ordination, and the structure that pays and houses them for life?

Ordained priesthood cannot be defined by how much of a person's time is spent working for the Church, for throughout history the Church has been supported by the faithful, time-consuming, unrewarded devotion of lay members. One might feel that one of the important functions of ordained priests is to provide professional rather than amateur worship which is dignified and beautiful enough to be a worthy offering to God. But much of that is done by musicians; and many a student service will be prepared with far more love and care than the services that are churned out for the fortieth year running by a poor tired run-down cleric. It is not even possible to define ordained priesthood in terms of those people who are paid by the Church, for there are many poor and needy people the world over for whom the Church, quite rightly, takes financial responsibility.

The trouble is that the only thing that uniquely defines ordained ministry, and therefore that ultimately substantiates the division between ordained and lay people, is the right to pronounce a handful of words: principally the absolution after confession, the blessing and the consecration prayer at the Eucharist. It is because uttering these words constitutes the only uniquely priestly function, that there is resistance to granting sacramental validity when they are not spoken by the ordained.

Sacraments, however, are not dependent on human rules but on divine grace. If the ordained priesthood is used as a way of limiting the sacraments this will impoverish Christians' experience of God and also diminish the effectiveness of the priests in ministering to the people. Jean Tillard claims that a priest only exists in his role at the Eucharist, where he concelebrates with the Christian community.[4] But if the whole community is concelebrating, then each is performing a priestly function and the ordained priest is doing nothing that is not effected by the other members.

Associated with these difficulties of defining the essence of priesthood, is the question of whether priesthood is functional or ontological. Some believe that one is a priest by virtue of the particular work that one is doing for some of the time, while others would hold that ordination bestows a unique status that cannot be taken away. Is someone a priest all the time, while mowing the lawn or cleaning their teeth, or only while performing certain functions such as celebrating the Eucharist or baptising? If it is all the time, then the performing of special functions in regard to the sacraments makes no difference to one's priesthood – one could be a priest for years without doing anything priestly. If, on the other hand, one is a priest only while performing these special functions, then any other people performing the same functions, regardless of whether or not they are ordained, would be priests. Whether one understands priesthood to be functional or ontological, there is no necessary connection between priesthood and sacraments.

There are a number of separate elements in the work and life of ordained priests. They are expected to imbibe, and then disseminate, theological education; they administer small businesses called churches; they are bound to provide worship and sacraments for the community; many of them are involved in charitable work, or at least visit the sick or bereaved of their congregation; in some country areas where the clergy are still considered to be local dignitaries, they even have social commitments to perform. But none of these roles, in themselves, even when closely engaged with the eucharistic elements, make priesthood a sacrament. Priesthood can only become a sacrament by virtue of what it is in itself; not because it is involved in sacramental activities. It is the sacramental nature of priesthood that we shall address in the following chapters.

Laity

Turning to the laity, the major disadvantage of the present understanding of priesthood is the fact that it disables a large majority of the personnel who are needed by the Christian Church to continue Christ's work on earth. Many lay people believe they are not qualified to instigate worship, to lead others to Christ, to bless, forgive or give thanks. Yet the Gospel message is clear, that Christ came to free all people, to help everyone to live more fully, to break down the barriers humanity had erected between itself and God, to bring in a commonwealth in which the least is the greatest and in which the veil of the temple has once and for all been torn in half. The laity *are* the Church, and an ordained priesthood only makes any sense within the context of that community of Christians.

It is unfortunate that the Second Vatican Council, for all the progress it made in recognising the importance of the faithful, still drew such a sharp distinction between clergy and laity: 'The hierarchy entrusts to the laity some functions which are more closely connected with pastoral duties, such as the teaching of Christian doctrine, certain liturgical actions, and the care of souls.'[5] It would be more accurate to say that the *laity* entrusts to the *clergy* some functions; for the Church is the whole people of God, not a clerical club, and it is really not up to a few individuals within the glorious company of God's people to decide how everyone else should live out their Christian vocations. St John the Divine writes in a different vein, describing his vision of the relationship Christ has with those whom he has called:

> with your blood
> you bought people for God
> of every race, language, people and nation
> and made them a line of kings and priests for God
> to rule the world. (Rev. 5:9–10)

It sometimes appears that the priesthood of all believers is the Church's best-kept secret. Few lay people are aware that they have been baptised into Christian priesthood, and even fewer would have any idea how they are meant to exercise that office in the world or in the Church.

While lay people are allowed to abdicate responsibility for evangelism, for handing down the faith from generation to generation, for building up the body of Christ in our own time and being a channel of sacramental grace, the Church will be impoverished and will appear increasingly irrelevant to the world. The expertise and sophistication of the whole Church must be harnessed if we are serious about working for a world in which the Gospel of Jesus Christ undergirds and blesses the whole of life.

That does not mean that every lay Christian should behave like an ordained priest. Exercising one's baptismal priesthood should not alter either the ordinariness of getting on with Christian life or the excitement of discovering the richness and significance of that life. But it does mean that each person has a responsibility to share, to lead, to create and build and to be the Church in the world. The response to anyone who asks a question such as: 'Why does the Church not do something about so and so?' is 'Yes, why don't you?'

If all are equal before God, then we are not constrained to accept that some are more equal than others. If God calls all the faithful to priesthood, then lay people are going to have to swallow the rough with the smooth and get on with the difficult business of living out their priesthood in the world. It is common, when the media want to know 'what the Church thinks' about a particular issue to turn to clergy as though they could adequately represent the Church. The ones who should represent the Church on such occasions are the people who sit in the pews on Sundays, who get teased for their faith at school or live out the Gospel for the poor in the bank, who comfort the troubled over coffee at the office or say their prayers on the commuter train, who convince the delinquent teenager of their human worth, face the tortured darkness of the mentally disturbed or share the fear of the old and dying while feeding them and changing the sheets. They are the ones who are the Church and who can truthfully represent the mind of that Church.

While the Church is identified with ordained priesthood, as it indisputably so often still is, it will fail to 'make disciples of all nations'. It is not reasonable to expect a small, ever-diminishing group of people to do that. The only chance is for lay Christians to consider it as part of their vocation in life; and that means living out their priesthood fully, not acting as monitors sent out by the real priests to do the tasks that they themselves have not time, or inclination, to do.

We have seen that in the early Church priesthood was not a special estate limited by training or ordination, but something to which all followers of Christ, our great high priest, were called. Our vocation and mission is to live Christ in the world: that just happens to be what Christianity is about. But unfortunately the structure that evolved over the years to help us to live out our calling succeeded in time in disabling the majority of those priests who call themselves lay members of the Church.

We cannot kid ourselves that we have got very far in fulfilling the mission given to us by Christ. Instead of the promised reign of God we have built a Church that looks to others like a minority club, and which fails, more often than not, to reflect God's love for the world. One of the major reasons for this failure is that we have continued to allow, even to foster, a deep distinction between sacred and secular which is contrary to the spirit of Christ. Furthermore, the traditional view of priesthood serves to exacerbate this false distinction.

One of the strengths of Vatican II was that it began to address this division between sacred and secular, and it is interesting that it did this through approaching the subject of the priesthood of the laity. First it was acknowledged that lay Christians are called to priesthood: 'They (laity) likewise exercise that priesthood by receiving the sacraments, by prayer and thanksgiving, by the witness of a holy life and by self-denial and active charity.'[6] But this priesthood is then differentiated from the ordained priesthood by being defined in exclusively non-ecclesiastical terms as belonging to the domain of the world, particularly in marriage and family life:

> In this way the lay person will throw himself wholly and energetically into the reality of the temporal order and effectively assume his role in conducting its affairs. At the same time, as a living member and witness of the Church, he will make the Church present and active in the midst of temporal affairs.[7]

Now if, as is surely indisputable, this holding together of Church and world is the responsibility of lay people, as part of the exercise of their priesthood, why is it not part of the priesthood of the ordained also? The implication seems to be that ordained clergy are set aside to concern themselves purely with the sacred. This is confirmed in the call for clergy to renounce the world, to cut themselves off from vast areas of normal human experience. Such an understanding of priesthood reinforces the very division between sacred and secular that the incarnation is meant to have scotched once and for all. This world is created by God and deemed to be good. It continues to be loved by God and was considered worthy of receiving God in the redemptive work of salvation. Who are we to separate off those bits which are suitable to qualify for Church and to label the rest as secular, outside the domain of the full-time clergy?

Yves Congar goes some way towards breaking down this false distinction in *Lay people in the Church*, where he denies any bland statement of division: 'Still less have we ever admitted the absurdly over-simplified formula, "Spiritual things appertain to the priest, temporal things to the layman" '.[8] But unfortunately he later falls into the trap of reinstating the very distinction he has rejected: 'God's purpose is not that there should be only a Church here below, but rather a Church *and* a world . . . These things can be done by lay people, for they belong both to the world and to the Church in a way that is true neither of clergy nor of monks.'[9]

The World Council of Churches made a real effort to avoid defining laity purely negatively as those who are not clergy; but even they, on occasion, have fallen into the trap of defining laity as those members of the Church who earn their daily bread by secular work and devote the greater part of their time to temporal occupation.

But what is secular occupation? Is the ordained priest, teaching in a seminary, or a missionary practising medicine in an underdeveloped country, or a nun offering hospitality or organising conferences, devoting his or her time to a spiritual occupation? Conversely, would it really be true to say that a mother, one of whose most diverse but time-consuming tasks is to bring up children 'in the faith and fear of the Lord', is engaged in a purely temporal occupation? Or the workman who lives in his community as a shining example of the love of God in action and so makes others pause to wonder at the reality of God? Or the teacher in a rough inner city school who sticks with the kids because she believes that they are precious to God, and gives them the benefit of the doubt when everyone else condemns them as worthless?

These occupations, surely, are every bit as spiritual as the professional lives lived by some ordained clergy who continue to draw their salaries from the Church while living lives of selfish idleness? The spiritual life is only of any value if it is *lived*. There is no part of the so-called temporal world where full-time priesthood cannot be exercised.

There is much fine literature on the subject of priesthood, and all Christians would benefit from reading it and applying it to their own situations. Michael Ramsey, for instance, in *The Christian Priest* defines a priest's intercession, very beautifully, as 'being with God with the people on our heart'.[10] But this is part of the essential duty of every Christian, not just of the ordained priest.

Of course, it is tempting for lay people to leave the difficult task of exercising priesthood to those who are paid to do it; but this will not do. The recommendations to ordained priests must also apply to lay priests. Similarly, exhortations to laity on how to live full Christian lives in the world must apply equally to ordained priests who, as members of the *laos*, are also called to be part of the commonwealth of God on earth. Only when we recognise our common priesthood will we be able to help each other to exercise that priesthood effectively.

In view of the dangers and difficulties that attend the ordained priesthood, could a case be made for advocating a revolution to throw the clergy out of the Church, like drones from a bee hive in autumn, and thus restore power to the people? Certainly if priesthood is confused with power and limited to the ordained ministry it could be argued that this would be the only reasonable course of action for the churches to take. But this would be to misunderstand and devalue the nature of priesthood. It is only by espousing a high doctrine of priesthood, understood as the priesthood of all believers, that ordination can be justified and can, indeed, represent an effective Christian sacrament.

A high doctrine of the priesthood of all believers does not diminish, though it does change, the role of the ordained priest. By allowing a sloppy doctrine of priesthood to evolve we have belittled an estate that should be one of the most vital and challenging commitments any man or woman could make, and one that would demand that they be deeply involved in the world rather than marginalised from it. Ordination to priesthood, properly understood, has nothing to do with guaranteeing meal tickets for life, or winning in a who-does-what dispute. Nor does it confer miraculous properties on the person who receives this vocation. For priesthood is meant to be a sacrament. As such, it should open our eyes to show us more of God, enable us to live in the divine light, help to bring in the promised reign of God.

9

Sacraments

To speak in the same breath of reforming our understanding of priesthood and of strengthening its sacramental quality is to court difficulty for, as we saw in chapter 7, the history of the Christian Church bears witness to the fact that reformers more often lose than enhance their participation in the sacraments. Why is it that so many of the movements of reformation moved away from the sacraments? Is it because there is something intrinsically wrong with our understanding of sacraments; or is it that this represents the area in which priestly power is most threatened?

To address this question it will be necessary to examine the major sacraments of the Church in order to see how each relates to the ordained priesthood and what we might mean by referring to the ordained priesthood in sacramental terms.

What is a sacrament?

A sacrament is defined as 'an outward and visible sign of an inward and spiritual grace given unto us',[1] and until late mediaeval times thirty or more sacraments were recognised. Peter Lombard, in his *Sentences*[2] restricted the list to seven, and these were the ones that were accepted by Thomas Aquinas and later affirmed by the Councils of Florence (1439) and Trent (1545–63).

The Anglican Church was later to accord special status to the two sacraments that were 'ordained of Christ our Lord in the Gospel': baptism and holy communion; and five other sacraments are recognised: confirmation, penance, orders, matrimony and extreme unction, somewhat dismissively referred to as 'five commonly called sacraments . . . which have not any visible sign or ceremony ordained of God'.[3] While it is undeniable that baptism and holy communion can be argued to arise as a direct result of the words of Jesus Christ recorded in the gospels, exactly how these two differ in practice from the other five tends to be left slightly hazy. In any case they are not unique, for Jesus clearly taught his disciples to anoint the sick as well.

The Church has never denied that other actions and events besides these seven could be sacramental, but it has chosen to define and limit *sacraments* to these particular channels of grace mediated through the Church. Sacraments are events, objects or actions which, though ordinary in themselves, speak to us forcefully of God or bring us to particularly vivid awareness of God's presence. The bearers of sacramental grace are not other-wordly objects like the sword Excalibur rising mysteriously from the lake, but ordinary things and relationships: like the bread we eat, the water in which we bathe, lovers with whom we want to share our lives. No magic is worked on these elements: just the reality of seeing them in God's truth.

For example, two people decide to marry. They believe they will love each other absolutely and eternally and through their love they begin to understand something of the tender, enduring, passionate love of God. So they enter the sacrament of marriage. The priest does not marry them, but in some way marks their marriage on behalf of the Church. Hence the affirmation in the Book of Common Prayer as the rings are exchanged: 'I thee wed.'

One might say the same about baptism: a particular way of life is chosen and marked symbolically, and the priest confirms that publicly on behalf of the Church. At the Eucharist, as we bring to mind the events of Christ's life, death and resurrection, we open ourselves to God, humbly accepting that life in God is about accepting, blessing, breaking and sharing. We take God into ourselves through the earthly symbols of bread and wine.

As with marriage, baptism, and Eucharist, so with ordination, the Church confirms what has become real in the life
of a particular Christian. Understood in this way, ordination
reflects more closely the experience and tradition of the early
Church, where it would appear that people were commissioned because of the gifts they displayed or services they
were already rendering in the community, rather than being
commissioned to undertake to display those gifts or render
those services. In this way, whatever ceremony or action
marked their appointment was naturally a sacramental recognition of the way in which the Holy Spirit was already
working in that person.

To view any of the sacraments as tricks performed by a
shaman figure is to diminish that sacrament; and to the
extent that we allow ourselves to forget this, we shall find
we have moved closer to folk religious superstition than to
true Christian understanding. All the sacraments are rooted
in the reality of ordinary life. What happens to these events
and objects when they become sacramental to us is similar
to what happens when we look at art. The piece of canvas
or the block of stone is not literally changed into something
else. Its material constitution is identical, but we are enabled,
through the ministration of the artist, to *see it as* a landscape,
a saint or a dancing woman.

While most people have, at some time, seen pictures in
the clouds, or in the flames of a fire, this is a faculty that
can be developed through frequent association with works
of art. In the same way, the more we can engage in the
kind of *seeing as* that reveals to us the nature of God, the more
enfolded and inspired we shall be by sacraments. Through
the sacraments, the Church helps to open our eyes to what
is already, and forever, true.

In *Life-Giving Spirit*[4] I described the sacramental quality
of some of the events and actions that are potentially available to many of us: parenthood, friendship, the sharing of
pain or beauty with another, experiences of hilarious
comedy, of dancing, of gardening. Such sacraments, like
those recognised by the Church, relate to those moments of
our lives when we become most deeply engaged with life. In

them and through them we pierce the veil and see more clearly into the nature of reality in God.

Quite ordinary things can be sacramental, and may sometimes be as effective as the sacraments in Church. For example, there is a sacrament that is celebrated daily by countless people who would consider themselves disqualified from giving absolution or blessing. While it is not a sacrament that is recognised by the Church, it is certainly the means of grace and forgiveness for those who receive it. It is what we might call the 'coffee cup confession'. In this sacrament something strengthening and comforting is shared, a person is given space and encouragement to speak the truth about their own pains and failings, and through the sharing and the being accepted in continued friendship, they know they are absolved.

Here, however, I shall concentrate on those sacraments that are generally recognised by the Church. These are sacraments that we share as members of the body of Christ; and the Church's role in these events and actions is an integral part of their meaning and power. But the fact that these sacraments are rooted in the worshipping community as the body of Christ, does not explain, or justify, the fact that all seven of them have become so clericalised that most people assume that no sacrament can be valid without the involvement of an ordained person.

The seven sacraments

Matrimony

Much debate has surrounded the sacrament of marriage, perhaps for the simple reason that marriages are commonly contracted by people regardless of whether they are churchgoers or not. Since the established Church of England, and to a lesser extent the Roman Catholic and Free Churches, became involved in the legal registration of marriage, as well as being bound up with many of the most picturesque and romantic images of weddings, the misconception arose that the sacrament of marriage is what takes place on one's wedding day, at a service in church. Further, since the law requires an authorised person to register the legal documentation of the marriage and this role is performed by the ordained, the sacrament is thought in some sense to be enacted or celebrated by that ordained person at that service.[5]

This is far from a true understanding of the sacrament of marriage, for in fact a wedding, however beautiful, is no more intrinsically a sacrament than is a Christmas carol service. The Church is at least partly to blame for the confusion, since it has failed to differentiate between the estate of marriage and the service at which the community gathers to 'witness the marriage of' those involved. To refer to this ceremony as a marriage is a misnomer: it is in fact a *wedding* service. Most languages, like English, do differentiate between weddings and marriages, which makes it all the more surprising that the two concepts should have become confused.

A wedding may mark the start of a sacramental marriage, but is not in itself the marriage. The sacrament that is recognised by the Church is the estate into which the man and woman enter, not the service they attend on their wedding day; and this sacrament is celebrated by the couple involved, not by the priest who officiates at their wedding. It could therefore be argued that priests are not necessary to validate the sacrament, even though, according to the law, marriages must be registered by someone in whom the State has invested the appropriate authority. If this is the case, then it must follow that it is not strictly necessary to be married in church to take part in the Christian sacrament of marriage.

It is, however, entirely natural that Christians should wish to celebrate the wonder of their love and union in the company of other Christians, to mark their changed status in the eyes of the world, to make promises that reflect the reality of their relationship now and into the future and to dedicate their new life together to God. To reassert the marriage as the sacrament, rather than the wedding, is not to diminish the importance of the event that takes two individuals and binds them legally and symbolically into a conjugal unit.

It is not surprising that people's primary pairing bond should come into the category of the sacramental, for sharing life and sex represent two points at which we are closest to the reality of who and what we are. It therefore appears that marriage is the only sacrament that is officially open to all, as long as they are not married already; but this is not strictly true, since in some denominations, such as in the Roman Catholic Church and in parts of the Orthodox Church, marriage is specifically *not* open to those who have been or wish to be ordained.[6] Is it, perhaps, significant, that the very hierarchies that have attempted to preserve the sacredness of sacraments by denying proper access to them to those outside their own group, should be the ones who do not share in the sacrament that would otherwise be open to all?

One way in which an attempt has been made to justify this position is by interpreting ordination as an alternative to marriage.[7] Under this interpretation, the priest, like the religious, cannot marry as he or she is already married in some special sense to God, or to the Church. By suggesting that marriage to God is an alternative to marriage to someone of the opposite sex, this interpretation of ordination diminishes marriage by implying both that normal marriage will always be a second best for a Christian and also that one cannot be totally committed (married) to God within a loving human marriage.

Although the Church pays lip-service to the estate of marriage, and certainly prefers matrimony to other relationships in which the partners are free to engage in sexual activity, the Christian community has a bad track record when it comes to honouring the sacrament of marriage. Many of the 'Church Fathers' were totally opposed to marriage, and the eventual outlawing of the married state to full-time Christian workers such as priests and religious indicates the low esteem in which the holy estate has been held by the religious hierarchy through history. Even today some religious leaders believe they have the right to legislate over the sexual practices of members, particularly, of course, in regard to measures taken to avoid conception during sexual intercourse.

Another example of the low esteem in which marriage has been held in certain sectors of the Church arises in the case of 'mixed marriages' between members of different denominations. It would be beyond belief if it were not so painfully true, that some priests, for instance in the Roman Catholic Church, consider they have the right to refuse to allow married couples to partake of the Eucharist together if one of the partners is not a member of that denomination. Perhaps more than any other single factor, this betrays the fact that marriage is not considered to be a sacrament, or if it is, to be a sacrament of a considerably lower order than holy communion. Either a sacrament is complete in itself and is a means of grace, a way of drawing aside the veil, or it is not; and if something *is* a sacrament, it cannot require another sacrament to validate it.

Even married couples who belong to denominations that claim to show more respect for the integrity and judgement of their members are unlikely to have found themselves upheld and supported in their marriages by an institutional Church that separates the sexes for as many ecclesiastical activities as possible. Few concessions are made to family life in the timetabling of meetings, in the ordering of services to take account of younger members, or in providing a forum in which people can discuss honestly and openly the marital and parental problems and opportunities faced by those who are engaged in ordinary occupations in the world. Given the Church's failure to educate its members in the significance of marriage, and the lack of preparation that is given to those embarking on this sacramental estate, it is not surprising that many find the struggle to understand and live out the sacrament so very difficult.

It is certainly the case that many weddings that do take place in church never lead in any real sense to sacramental marriage. It must also be admitted that although the Church has set controls on who may be married in Church, the sacrament of marriage is just as much open to those who are denied access to a church wedding as to those who qualify for one.

I have discussed the sacrament of marriage at some length because marriage and Eucharist are the two sacraments that have been most real in my own life; in other words they have worked as sacraments because through them more of the mysterious reality of God has been revealed to me. Others who, because of the particular circumstances of their lives, have responded more fully to other sacraments, would no doubt choose different emphases in addressing the theme of sacraments.

Baptism

There are branches of the Christian Church where baptism is the most important sacrament, and with good reason. There is more evidence for its practice as a rite in the early Church than there is for other sacraments; and the charge laid on the missionary Church was to go and baptise, not offer holy communion. Churches are divided over what age people should be before being baptised and whether total immersion or affusion (sprinkling) should mark the occasion, but none of the mainstream denominations would deny that baptism in one form or another is the sacrament of initiation into the congregation of the faithful.

The many Christians who practise infant baptism would argue that through it the Church makes it clear that grace is freely given, rather than earned. God takes the initiative and the baby is welcomed into the Church by the community before he or she can play a part in that decision. The strength of this argument is that it brings out the *community* aspect of the sacraments; although, sadly, it has to be recognised that many family baptisms then go against the spirit of this community endeavour by arranging private ceremonies of baptism for their offspring, outside the normal congregational life of the Church.

Other denominations insist that baptism should be reserved for those who have reached an age of discretion.[8] Although most associated with branches of the Church that do not in general practise adult baptism, I must admit that I consider the case for adult baptism to be overwhelming. Baptised as an infant, I played no active part in my own baptism and cannot remember this seminal event in my life. When I returned to the fold after adolescent rebellion and exploration there was no ritual to mark my new commitment or recognise a more mature approach to the life of faith and prayer. My re-immersion into the Christian faith bore many of the marks of re-birth, yet, as far as I was concerned, logic forbade the possibility of a second baptism. In this, at least, I was consistent with the Book of Common Prayer, in which each of the baptism services can commence only when it has been affirmed that the person has not been baptised before. The Roman Catholic Church, too, explicitly denies the possibility of partaking of this sacrament more than once: 'To imprint a character upon the soul which cannot be effaced, thus making it impossible for this sacrament to be repeated.'[9]

This 'one-off' quality of baptism raises interesting questions about sacraments in general. A Christian can take communion several times a week, confess sins and be absolved when the need arises, experience the estate of marriage in the daily rhythm of faithfulness and passion, but once one is baptised it is assumed that the deed is done and one bears the mark of it for ever. The fact that many people do not know whether or not they were baptised as infants, and certainly have nothing to show for it, diminishes the sense and importance of the sacrament and risks bringing all the sacraments into disrepute.

The meaning and significance of baptism is based on our entering into life in Christ; but a baby cannot do that, and no parents can do it for their child. Parents might make a public confession of their thanks for the child; they might present their baby for blessing or express their hopes that the child will grow up into the faith and love of God; they might claim some sort of church membership for their child, welcoming him or her into the family of the Church, or make their own commitment to raise the child in a Christian home. All those intentions and emotions are worthy, and all can be the basis for some kind of public affirmation or ritual – or even sacrament; but none of them constitutes baptism.[10]

The only model of baptism that can claim New Testament validity is the baptism entered into by someone who, to the best of his or her ability and understanding at that time, makes a personal commitment to Christ. Yet the Book of Common Prayer makes no excuse or apology for insisting that the younger the child is presented for baptism the better:

> The Ministers of every Parish shall often admonish the people that they bring their children to Baptism as soon as possible after birth, and that they defer not the Baptism longer than the fourth, or at furthest the fifth, Sunday unless upon a great and reasonable cause.[11]

There was a time when Christians could undertake baptism on behalf of someone else and it was not uncommon for people to avail themselves of this facility to baptise their dead relations by proxy. Such superstitious practices are now frowned upon, and yet most of the churches continue to imply that it is perfectly sensible for parents to present babies for baptism before they are at an age when they can have any awareness, let alone understanding or approval, of what is going on. Veiled threats about eternal damnation for those poor innocents who die before being baptised only serve to further confuse the issue of what baptism is and entails.

There are few more urgent longings that Christian parents have for their children than that they should grow up into the Christian faith, to enter into personal relationship with the God of love and to experience something of the riches of spiritual joy for themselves. But it does not require very much wisdom to understand that although parents can provide a loving and Christ-centred home, can undertake to educate young children in 'the faith and fear of the Lord', offer an example of what the Christian life is about and instil good habits in their children as early as possible, they cannot at the end of the day choose their children's faith or commit them to membership of any church. All they can do is give thanks when they see their children finding their own path to Christ.

A reassessment of priesthood is bound to lead to questioning and analysis of the other sacraments, and this is particularly so in the case of baptism through which the faithful are initiated into that Christian priesthood which is a necessary part of full membership of the Church. If baptism as practised in the New Testament brings all the rights of membership and priesthood in the Christian Church, is infant baptism one of the ways in which an hierarchical priesthood has maintained control and supremacy, devaluing baptism from a well-prepared initiation sacrament into a blessing and naming ceremony for babies? In this shift, the sacramental emphasis has moved from the one being baptised, to the person of the priest, who undertakes to do something *for* or *to* the child, rather than assisting the candidate to understand and enact the sacrament in such a way that life in Christ is celebrated and strengthened.

All baptised Christians are, in fact, qualified to baptise on occasions, for 'In view of the importance of Baptism for salvation, in the absence of a priest or deacon, when there is danger of death, anyone may and must baptize.'[12] The Anglican rubrics reiterate this charge: 'In an emergency a lay person may be the minister of baptism, and should subsequently inform those who have the pastoral responsibility for the person so baptized.'[13] The Alternative Service Book goes on to explain the procedure if the person thus baptised in an emergency survives. While it is deemed necessary that the person, or in the case of infant baptism the parents of the child, should on a later occasion go through the part of the baptism service in which credal assent is given, there is no question of blessing the water again, or of marking the person with the sign of the cross in the name of the Father, Son and Holy Spirit. In other words, any Christian not only may, but should, baptise in an emergency; and that sacrament of baptism is valid.

However, if baptism by a lay person works sometimes, in an emergency, it must work always. Either one can perform an effective sacrament or one cannot. It simply is not rational to suggest that the same person is on some occasions enjoined to perform actions and say words that constitute a sacrament and on other occasions is disqualified from saying those same words and performing those same actions. This also applies to other sacraments celebrated by lay people in response to emergency situations. If they are valid when convenient, they are potentially valid always.

Confirmation

It was because of infant baptism that the need for confirmation arose. If baptismal vows were made on the child's behalf, without consultation or agreement, then it was clearly necessary for the child to confirm those vows for himself or herself at some later stage. In a way, confirmation came to take the place of proper baptism, with the candidate's public affirmation and willingness to be filled with the Holy Spirit. Confirmation did not use the external sign of water associated with traditional baptism, but satisfied something of the same need in the newly aware Christian to make a public affirmation a part of their initiation into full membership of the Christian Church.

With time, however, confirmation has suffered from the same process as has baptism, for in many churches there has been an increasing tendency to confirm young; taking pre-adolescents, before they have had time or opportunity to test their faith, and encouraging them to assent to promises that they are unlikely to be able to honour as they pass through the stormy waters of adolescence. This trend towards catching people young betrays a lack of confidence in what the Church has to offer, for it assumes that unless one can persuade someone to join the Church before they wander from the fold, they are unlikely to want to join of their own accord later.

One disadvantage of confirmation, at whatever age, is the fact that it affiliates a person to a particular church in a way that baptism does not. So, while one is baptised into the Christian Church more or less regardless of denomination, confirmation has more the character of taking out club membership. However, a more serious disadvantage of early confirmation is that it leaves adults with no meaningful sacrament of identification with the Church. It is important that young people passing from childhood to adulthood move from unquestioning dependency to mature decision-making and personal conviction. Such a process frequently involves questioning, rebellion and at times outright rejection.

As the teenage years of exploration and doubt draw to a close it is not uncommon for the most rebellious of teenagers to be deeply and irresistibly attracted to the Christian faith and for some that will mean returning to the bosom of their own or another church tradition. This is the point at which a meaningful initiation sacrament is needed, and many young Christians have felt the lack of any way in which to mark their personal return to faith or their re-entry, as responsible and contributing adults, into the Christian Church.

There is certainly a need for sacraments that are available to children and young people, who can respond passionately and sensitively to the spiritual life. But to push baptism and confirmation earlier and earlier does not really answer this need, and threatens to devalue sacraments that are for the nourishment and growth of all Christians, not just the young.

If the churches do wish to keep the dual process of baptism and confirmation, then some of the difficulties can be overcome by baptising children when they are old enough to assent to the decision and to take an active part in preparing for the sacrament. As has long been the practice in the Roman Catholic Church, children can then be prepared for first communion, possibly in their early teens, so that they can, if they choose, have access to this means of grace as they explore their faith and discover the need to deepen their relationship with God. Confirmation could then be delayed until adulthood, when it can be a true confirming of the vows made earlier. The Methodist Church goes some way towards meeting this need in its annual Covenant service; and it not surprising that this treasure of Methodism is often welcomed so warmly by other denominations when they meet it through their involvement in ecumenical projects.

Penance, or the forgiveness of sins

There are two points during a celebration of the Eucharist in an Anglican church at which it is mandatory that the words should be spoken by an ordained priest. One of these is the prayer of consecration, which we shall consider in the next chapter; the other is the absolution. Part of the mystique of priesthood has long been bound up with the tradition that it is the priest and the priest alone who can, on God's behalf, absolve people from their sins.

This tradition has some scriptural authority, stemming from the words in the sparse and contracted Johannine account of Pentecost in which Jesus says:

> Receive the Holy Spirit.
> For those whose sins you forgive,
> they are forgiven;
> for those whose sins you retain,
> they are retained. (John 20:22, 23)

However, St John sets these words in the context of Jesus coming to the room where the disciples are gathered for fear of the Jews. It is not the twelve who are said to be in hiding, but a group of disciples which would have included some of the twelve; though we know from the succeeding verses that one at least, Thomas, was not present on this occasion. The charge to forgive sins, therefore, was not specific to the twelve but was given to all who followed Jesus.

The insight that forgiveness is vital to the life and health of a community must have been valuable to the early Christians learning to live close to each other, and would benefit the Church today far more than clerical-dependent forms of confession and absolution. We know that it is necessary for emotional health that people do not carry burdens of guilt. In a loving community, family, congregation or group of friends, an important part of living out God's love is to know and forgive each other, to trust others to accept and love us as we really are.

Christians often appear to be as keen to refuse to acknowledge the reality of sin as anyone else. We excuse ourselves and fail to accept responsibility for the things we have thought, said or done that are unworthy of our calling. Sacramental confession should provide the opportunity for us to face up to the reality of our sin. It is not mawkish, and certainly should not instil feelings of guilt since we know before we start that we are forgiven.

In the context of a marriage, family or loving Christian community, we can confess to each other and be reassured that we are accepted and loved. But when modern life removes us from such communities, we may well need a more formal way of responding to this human need, and value the opportunity to 'make our confession'. In such circumstances, the priest, or the community of Christians, fulfils the function of a good marriage, friendship or family. It is also, no doubt, sometimes a help to confess to someone who is right outside the immediate situation with which one is struggling. In the same way, counselling has become a part of late twentieth-century reality, particularly for those who, for one reason or another, have been deprived of the basic human right of being in honest, loving and accepting communion with another.

When the priest absolves the congregation at the Eucharist, he or she is not forgiving the people, but assuring them of God's forgiveness. We do all need to be reminded of this, particularly when we feel really bad about our failure to live life as God intended; and a prime task of any Christian in communion with others is to carry that charge of reminding others that they are known, forgiven and loved by God.

We can only actually forgive a person for the wrongs they have done to us, and it is as important for our soul's health as for theirs that we do that. But we can also, and more generally, proclaim God's forgiveness, because we have been charged to do so; and this task, either within the context of the Eucharist or in the privacy of shared confidences, is the responsibility and right of all Christians. In this role we are not intermediaries, but reassurers; and in the absence of anyone else to fulfil this function it is important that a priest or other representative of the Church should do it.

This interpretation of Christ's command would appear to

be the one that was current in the early Church, for we read
in the Letter of James:

> Confess your sins to one another, and pray for one
> another, and this will cure you ... if one of you strays
> away from the truth, and another brings him back to it,
> he may be sure that anyone who can bring back a sinner
> from the wrong way that he has taken will be saving a
> soul from death and covering up a great number of sins.
> (5:16, 19–20)

In this way the early Christians were living out their understanding of Jesus Christ as the new covenant. There was no
necessity to go to a priest to confess and be absolved; sins
were to be confessed to each other. Those who followed
Christ were called to forgive those who sinned against them,
and to assure all who were sorry for their sins that they were
cleared in the sight of God.

Anointing

We have seen how the writer of the Letter of James connected
the idea of confession and forgiveness to that of healing. The
final sacrament is one whose nature has changed in recent
years, moving from being called extreme unction or last rites
– which like penance was concerned with confession and
absolution – to the anointing of the sick, with the emphasis
on healing. This understanding of anointing is not new in
the Orthodox Church, where at vespers it is common for all
members of the congregation to be anointed.

With the evolution of this sacrament in the Western
churches in recent years, it has taken on a clearer identity
and, it could be argued, begun to be celebrated as a sacrament in its own right, rather than as an adjunct to other
sacraments (such as penance and holy communion) on certain occasions.

When this sacrament was administered only to those who
were thought to be on the point of death, it performed the
role of last confession so that the dying person could be
entirely absolved before death. The Second Vatican Council
moved the emphasis away from the forgiveness of sins

towards healing, and the sacrament therefore became appropriate for the ill as much as for the dying.[14] At the same time it ceased to be the purely private affair that was necessary for a final confession; and as family members, doctors, nurses and close friends began to attend, it became a sacrament more firmly tied into the community.[15]

This is far more in keeping with the commissioning and activity of the first missionary disciples that we read about in St Mark's gospel. 'So they set off to preach repentance; and they cast out many devils, and anointed many sick people with oil and cured them' (6:12–13). It is an inescapable fact that the early Church was involved in healing and, like Jesus, gave high priority to this element of ministry. Francis MacNutt has written extensively on healing and its place in the Church today, and in *Healing* he traces examples of anointing for healing being undertaken by lay people throughout the early centuries until at least the twelfth century.[16] He concludes that there is no reason why lay people should not perform this ministry today; and in fact the Old Roman Ritual gives a blessing of oil for ordinary use, which could easily be adapted for this purpose.[17]

It is not difficult to see why the association grew up between anointing and death. In several cultures dead bodies were, and are, anointed for burial. It was also common in Middle Eastern countries to be anointed before a journey, possibly originally as a protection against sun and wind: and death is the longest journey. The woman with the alabaster jar who, in Matthew's and Mark's gospels poured precious ointment over the head of Jesus, is said by Jesus to have anointed him in preparation for his burial.

Although the story of the anointing of Jesus's feet is more commonly known, both Matthew and Mark state quite categorically that it was his head that was anointed, and only St John's gospel speaks of the woman anointing his feet. It is, perhaps, both striking and significant that in general the Church, which has associated the anointing of the head with priesthood, is more comfortable with the idea of a woman anointing the feet than the head of Jesus (Matt. 26; Mark 14; John 12). If a woman, within first century Middle Eastern culture, could legitimately anoint the Son of God, it is reasonable to conclude that there is no reason why any Christian should not anoint anyone else.

However, healing the sick is not the only function of anointing, which also carries connotations of joy, blessing, beauty and making something special. For the psalmists anointing with oil was associated with joyful occasions, and Psalm 45 speaks of the 'oil of gladness':

That is why God, your God, has anointed you
with the oil of gladness, above all your rivals;
myrrh and aloes waft from your robes.(v. 7)

Psalm 23, too, in celebrating the goodness of God, includes amongst the other blessings not just a table bounteously laden and a cup brimming over, but a head anointed with oil. Such anointing was a common gesture of hospitality in this ancient culture, and indicated to the guest that they were special and welcome. Kings were (and are) anointed with oil at their consecration; priests at their ordination. In anointing a person with oil one affirms in a public and sensuous way their value.

The word 'Christ', like 'Messiah', means 'the anointed one'; so when we are anointed we in a sense 'become Christ' and enter into union with him. Interpreted like this, the sacrament should be seen as a vital part of Christian experience. In anointing a person we mark their specialness, and even if the person is dying this affirmation goes with them.

We have recognised with the other sacraments how it is basic to their very nature that the ordinary things of life are taken and blessed and, perceived in a new way, become channels of God's grace to us. It is easy to see this in the case of holy communion and baptism, but the same applies with unction, for the two elements used in this sacrament are oil and human touch. Oil was a commodity much used in ancient times, both medically and for personal grooming and comfort. In recent years some of the functions and pleasures of oil have been rediscovered with the re-emergence of body oils, massage oil, bath oil and essential oils. As in former times the oils soothe and protect and often impart pleasing smells. Added to touch, as for instance in massage, they can bring physical relief from pain and endue a person with a sense of well-being.

Touch, too, is important to the sacrament of anointing. Most people are fairly sensitive to the different ways in which they can be touched: roughly, aggressively, tenderly, erotically, predatorily, medically. In the sacrament, the person who anoints allows his or her hands to be used to convey care and respect for the person being anointed, and in this way the ordinary element of human touch is blessed and used as a channel of grace.

Jesus knew the importance of touch, which he used to good effect in several of his miracles of healing. The really striking aspect of his treatment of lepers, and the one that broke through their barrier of pain and rejection, was the fact that Jesus was prepared to touch them. In healing the man born blind, too, Jesus knows that with the sense of sight missing, touch becomes all the more vital. There are many in the world and in the Church today who are suffering from the lack of close human contact. Perhaps if we were to use touch sacramentally we should begin to witness miracles of healing at many different levels.

In examining some of the sacraments that the Church has set aside as special means of grace, we have seen how none of these events genuinely requires the presence or involvement of an ordained priest. The sticking point for most branches of the Church, however, has always been the celebration of holy communion; so it is to that pivotal sacrament that we turn in the next chapter, before considering the sacrament of ordination itself.

10

Eucharist

Eucharist in the Christian Church

Unlike, say, belief in the Holy Trinity, adherence to eucharistic worship has not generally been a defining factor in what constitutes a Christian church; and many Christians, such as those who belong to the Religious Society of Friends or to the Salvation Army, do not have or desire access to this particular sacrament.

For Quakers, in the same way that it is not necessary or desirable to celebrate the feasts of Christmas and Easter, since every day is a celebration of the incarnation and resurrection; so holy communion as a service has no place, since Christ enjoined us to 'remember' every time we eat and drink.[1] For Christians, they assert, every meal is, in effect, a re-enactment of the Last Supper. If all Christians reflected that awareness in their ordinary lives, the truth and power of the Eucharist might be released to have more impact on the Church and in the world.

Friends' testimony is to a corporate life and experience of God which does not depend on the observance of outward sacraments. Abstaining from the outward sacraments does not inevitably follow from this, but is one way of witnessing to it, particularly when the importance of the outward sacraments in building up the life of the church is being stressed.[2]

However, the fact remains that, for the majority of Christians, some form of eucharistic communion is at the centre of their understanding of their Christian life and worship;

and the re-enactment of the Last Supper has, under a variety of names, been the central liturgical and devotional act for most Christian churches throughout the ages.

The particular sequence of words and actions that make up our 'remembrance' speaks, and has always spoken, to the soul of many of those who try to follow Jesus Christ. Through communion, Christians through the ages have found a way to enter into Christ's passion, his life, death and resurrection. And in doing this they have been enabled, despite the infinite variety of their circumstances, characters, ideologies and levels of theological understanding, to make sense of their own experience. The bread of their everyday lives, the wine of their greatest joy and deepest pain, are offered up to become the body and blood of Jesus Christ.

For century after century, spreading slowly to every continent and country and among every race on earth, this action has been done, in every conceivable human need from infancy and before it to extreme old age and after it, from the pinnacles of earthly greatness to the refuge of fugitives in caves and dens of the earth. Men have found no better thing than this to do for kings at their crowning and for criminals going to the scaffold; for armies in triumph or for a bride and bridegroom in a little country church; for the proclamation of a dogma or for a good crop of wheat; for the wisdom of the Parliament of a mighty nation or for a sick old woman afraid to die; for a schoolboy sitting an examination or for Columbus setting out to discover America; for the famine of whole provinces or for the soul of a dead lover; in thankfulness because my father did not die of pneumonia; for a village headman much tempted to return to fetish because the yams had failed; because the Turk was at the gates of Vienna; for the repentance of Margaret; for the settlement of a strike; for a son for a barren woman; for Captain so and so, wounded and prisoner of war; while lions roared in the nearby amphitheatre; on the beach at Dunkirk; while the hiss of scythes in the thick June grass came faintly through the windows of the church; tremulously, by an old monk on the fiftieth anniversary of his vows; furtively by an exiled bishop who had hewn timber all day in a prison camp near Murmansk; gorgeously, for the canonisation of S. Joan of Arc – one could fill many pages with the reasons why men have done this and not tell a hundredth part of them. And best of all, week by week, and month by month on a hundred thousand successive Sundays, faithfully, unfailingly, across the parishes of christendom, the pastors have done just this.[3]

Mass, the Eucharist, Holy Communion, the Lord's Supper, love feast: the names vary, but the depth of the experience for the adherents is the same. For some, the Eucharist is so vital that they do all in their power to take it as often as possible, preferably every day. For others it is so special that it should be rarely experienced and then only after extensive preparation. But in each case the one who is privileged to take part in this sacrament re-aligns her or his life with Christ's, is able to rise after receiving the body and blood of Christ, filled with God and bearing that God-life in the world. At that point it is inappropriate to bow to the altar or to anything else on earth. For, absolved through Christ's sacrifice and made one with Christ through taking his body and blood into ourselves, for a few brief moments we can stand before God in the dignity of our full humanity redeemed by Christ.

This holy and life-giving sacrament, however, carries a sting in its tail; for, far from uniting Christians, the Eucharist has been more divisive than any other aspect of Christian belief and practice. Even today, after years of ecumenical activity and advance, Christians of some of the different denominations, who may love and respect each others' traditions, who often work together to bring in the reign of God and experience the unity of Christ in their common lives, are officially forbidden to share communion together. As we have noted in chapter nine, for some this is even the case when they are joined together in the sacrament of marriage. In the interweaving of their lives they may discover and embody the love of God, but when they go to church together, they cannot share in the body and blood of Christ.

Faced with this deep, sinful scar at the heart of our religious life, it is no wonder that many turn away from the Church. This refusal to recognise the validity of the sacraments in different traditions is not an incompatibility of belief on behalf of those who partake of the sacrament, but one of the manifestations of the clerical power that threatens to rob the heart of the Church of its life. It is arguable that even the great debate over consubstantiation or transubstantiation was something of a red herring, more divisive in the misinterpretation of each position than in underlying belief. The doctrines impinged little on the faithful who attended and were fed by the Eucharist, and the philosophy behind transubstantiation has altered significantly over the years, with the result that it would be well-nigh impossible to slip a wafer between the eucharistic theology of most Protestants and Roman Catholics.

Safeguarding the holy

The sacraments are the life-blood of the Christian Church: the spring from which flows all our being and living in the world; the sea into which we feed all that we are and do. In the sacraments, however, and perhaps especially in the Eucharist, the Church attempts, against the odds, to limit and control the religious experience of her adherents. Many suspect that it is because of the power of the Holy Spirit challenging and inspiring people, that such control is only absolute where conformity or apathy rule. Some control of the holy is undeniably desirable, and due consideration should be given to finding appropriate ways in which safeguards and correctives might be achieved; but all too often it is assumed that control of religion is the prerogative of the clergy, and has something to do with power.

To be fair, it should be admitted that there are offshoots of the Church where this does not apply, such as in the case of the Brethren Church in which any member can celebrate the sacraments. But so deep is the assumption of clerical control over the Eucharist in the Anglican Church, for instance, that the hierarchies are more ready to countenance so-called 'extended communion', so maintaining control over the consecration of the elements, than to encourage the priesthood of all believers to take this message and this sacrament out into all the world. Even more reprehensibly, it would appear that in the Sydney diocese of Australia the appeal of lay presidency at the Eucharist stemmed at least in part from the fact that it could be used as a let-out in order to bar women from the priesthood.

So absolute has this power become, that the Church has allowed clergy to control not only who may officiate at the service, but who may receive the sacraments. The qualifications vary: sometimes there is an insistence that potential recipients must have fasted for a certain length of time, or abstained from sexual intercourse; for some, such as the divorced and remarried, they are barred from receiving the sacraments for many years: for others it is required that they have recently made a formal confession. Faced with the searing holiness and goodness of God, none of us is worthy to share the feast; but within that vast and unscaleable unworthiness, small variations based on personal morality or religious practices fade into utter irrelevance. When God has given all, far beyond our deserving, who are we to withhold that grace from one another or even, in the extreme, to inflict on another human being the ultimate pain of excommunication?

Other than the injunction that we should 'do this in memory of me', Jesus gave only one clear instruction that has bearing on our conduct at holy communion: 'If you are bringing your offering to the altar and there remember that your brother has something against you, leave your offering there before the altar, go and be reconciled with your brother first, and then come back and present your offering (Matt. 5:23–24). That is why confession and absolution play such an important role in the Eucharist. It also explains why the Peace, only fully and actively reinstated in the liturgical reforms of the twentieth century, is an essential part of the sacraments and not an optional extra for the extroverted or friendly.

Confession and absolution, of course, are not necessarily the same thing as reconciliation, and it might be considerably easier for the Church to mete out words of forgiveness on behalf of God than to effect true reconciliation among people. In this regard it is noteworthy that as part of the post-Vatican II enlightenment, the Roman Catholic Church reformed its approach to the sacrament of penance, putting the emphasis on the community aspect of the service, and even re-naming it the sacrament of reconciliation.

It is abundantly clear that priests were not given any function at the Last Supper by Christ, or instructed to play a role by Paul when he set out the tradition to which Christians should adhere at communion (1 Cor. 11.23–27). When, probably for good practical reasons, priests emerged in the Christian Church, it was not to celebrate holy communion, for Christ's sacrifice had done away with the need for priests to offer sacrifice. It was the whole community that became the body of Christ, and therefore able, as a body, to re-enact and celebrate that perfect sacrifice. Any leaders should be *enabling* the whole people to do that, not abrogating power and responsibility to themselves.

The Eucharist, like the other sacraments, is a public action; and whoever celebrates the sacrament does so on behalf of the Church. Ideally it is not something that can be enacted by one person alone, even though there have been plenty of cases of abuse of this principle. A celebration of the Eucharist is not a private devotion – there are other forms of devotion for individuals, and some forms of prayer and worship are better done alone. If, because of unfortunate isolating circumstances, it is impossible to be with other people, anyone who seeks to take part in this communal activity of the Church must somehow be at least imaginatively joined to a wider community.

Christ, of course, did it alone. But it is *we* who are called to be the body of Christ, not *I*. As the body of Christ, we live out his priesthood, but this is something we do as a community, a royal nation, not as individuals. Therefore, far from arguing that only priests can celebrate the Eucharist, it would be more theologically accurate to insist that no one single person can ever celebrate alone.

Despite this, it is one of the most intractable assumptions of many branches of the Christian Church that only ordained people can celebrate the Eucharist. Cases can be quoted of communities in remote areas where communion has been given only on the rare occasions that a priest has visited. There are many rural parishes where there are not enough priests to go round and where the whole congregation is deprived of the Eucharist for weeks on end. There are communities of nuns which are constrained to wheel on a tame secular priest, who does not and cannot share intimately in the religious life of their community, to do for them what they could far better do themselves; and when he (or, rarely, she) goes on holiday they have to manage without or share the reserved sacrament.

What shaky, empty eucharistic theology is operating, which does not allow a community of deeply religious sisters, or even the mother superior, to celebrate? These women are living daily as priests in the world; presenting that world to Christ and Christ to that world; feeding and enabling other Christians in their spiritual life. But in order to receive the sacrament they must import an ordained priest to celebrate for them, regardless of whether that priest is senile, adulterous, full of hatred or in the process of losing the faith. Further, because they live under a vow of obedience to the Church, these are the very people who are least likely to challenge the system.

Faced with these blaring injustices and attempts to constrict the life blood of the Christian life, it is laughable that the Church should have spent so much time in recent years squabbling about whether women, or homosexuals, or the divorced, can be ordained. More fundamental issues of priesthood are crying out to be addressed.

The Eucharistic age

This iniquity has become more apparent as the Eucharist has increased in popularity as the core of Christian worship. Demand for the Eucharist increased exponentially as other services, such as matins and evensong, became less popular. A fair hypothesis is that as words crumbled (as words must if they are not renewed and revitalised), actions, particularly symbolic actions, became vital. For many Christians their participation in Holy Communion is the core of their whole religious life, and is meaningful, inspiring, life-enhancing and sacramental, regardless of the suitability of, or even their personal relationship with, the person who happens to be celebrating.

The Church accepts that the efficacy of the sacrament is not dependent upon the one who celebrates. Many ordained priests have led lives of selfishness and sin, but when they celebrate the Eucharist they can still, miraculously, be a means of grace. But it is God's grace, and the power of the sacrament, that effects this, not the ordination service; and the same should apply to any member of the royal priesthood who acts within and on behalf of the Church.

During the twentieth century there has been an increasing emphasis on the Eucharist in many of the mainstream churches: with Roman Catholics worshipping in the vernacular and increasingly receiving in both kinds (that is, personally receiving both bread and wine), Anglicans reforming their liturgies and developing the discipline of regular communion, and many Nonconformist churches responding to the yearning for the beauty of the sacraments among their congregations.

However, rather than the increase in sacramental worship leading to an empowering of the priesthood of believers, the role of the laity has diminished still further. When communion was a rare event, the religious life of the parish could continue without the need for clergy to administer regular sacraments; but now that there is an expectation that every parish church will at the very least have one celebration of the Eucharist each week, clergy have become more essential to the continuing life of the Church.

Most denominations have some form of subsidiary leadership in the church, such as local preachers or elders in the Nonconformist churches, lay readers in the Anglican Church and eucharistic ministers in the Roman Catholic Church. In the Anglican Church, however, not even a lay reader, who has received training and been licensed, can stand in for the clergy to celebrate the Eucharist. The order of readers in the Church of England was developed at a time when matins and evensong were the most popular services, and readers were needed to take some of these services in order to relieve the parish clergy. Even if the parish priest had to be absent for an extended period the reader could carry on saying the offices and preaching.

Readers are still allowed to lead public worship, read the gospel, lead the people in prayer and preach the word of God. But now that the Eucharist has taken over as the fundamental service of the Church, inelligibility to celebrate the sacrament renders the office of reader more incidental. This is, perhaps, all the more strange since it is considerably easier to train people to preside at holy communion than to give them theological training for preaching.

Matins and evensong have now almost disappeared in some areas, while there is a greater demand for communion than the diminishing body of ordained priests can satisfy. One response to this situation might be for the Church of England to adapt the duties of readers, who have already received training and been formally recognised by the Church, and to license them to celebrate the Eucharist.

However, sensible as this change would be – and if it were implemented immediately it would certainly solve some of the problems of too few clergy – it is only a partial answer and in itself would perpetuate the wrong understanding that is disabling and diminishing the Church. For it would be to professionalise a further class of people in the Church, rather than to release the Church to receive the ministry of the whole priesthood of believers. Such a further professionalisation would ultimately be worse than useless: it would exacerbate the already rampant tendency to disable the royal priesthood which is the body of Christ on earth, the Church.

It certainly does not require three or more years of training for a Christian to learn to celebrate the Eucharist; and theological training, in any case, does not guarantee that the sacraments will be celebrated well. It is, however, important that the Eucharist, as the Church's central act of worship, should be subject to various controls. It is not something that anyone can do, for it is essential to its nature that those who take part in it do so as the community of Christians. It should be recognised as that activity by others and in some way represent the whole Church, however many or few people take part in that particular re-enactment.

The sacred is, and probably should be, always hedged round with safeguards, though the reasonable care that we take to avoid casting our pearls before pigs should not be taken so far that it threatens to reinstate the temple curtain. Nor is the fact that safeguards are desirable any excuse for stultifying the form of the Eucharist, or caging it so that it cannot grow or reflect the local or temporary circumstances of a particular group of people. But it does mean that holy communion should not be treated as a mix and match service, a human sandwich with extra sacramental relish thrown in.

Words can change, emphases can vary, but the Eucharist is about certain events remembered and celebrated in the light of world history and the revelation of a Church that has continued down the ages. When this supremely important activity is performed by a human being on behalf of other people, it should be executed to a high standard, in comprehensible and audible language, with attention to the holiness and significance of the actions, and with respect for those who share the sacrament with them.

The nature of the sacrament of holy communion

Paul picks out the essential features of the Eucharist in 1 Corinthians 11:23–27 and, as this was the pattern that he

set before the early Church to direct their practice, it is
worth taking note of these basics:

• *On the night he was betrayed*

What happened took place within the context of ordinary
life. It was not a sign given by Jesus after his Resurrection
and Ascension, but something that was meaningful at the
depths of his humanity, when one of his closest friends was
planning to betray him and bring about his humiliation and
painful death.

• *the Lord Jesus took some bread*

This was not sanctified temple bread, but the ordinary
bread that was lying around on the table. It was not something Jesus miraculously produced for them, like manna in
the wilderness, or even surprising like the bread at the feeding of the five thousand. That group of people had *already*
been sharing this bread together.

• *after he had given thanks*

The ordinary was recognised as coming from God. Thankfulness is always the core emotion in the Eucharist, and
therefore in life as well. Jesus, as he saw ahead to the inevitable outcome of his mission, thanked God for all that was
and would be.

• *he broke it*

Only that which is broken can be shared. Christ himself was
to be broken in love; those who followed him were to be
broken in love. Fallen humanity is broken, but in its very
brokenness is sanctified and given.

• *This is my body, which is for you*

In the sacrament we are able to see into the true significance
of things. The bread is bread: it is also the body of Christ,
and through it we continue to be blessed and broken as the
body of Christ on earth, in order to feed the world and to
unveil the significance of life. Reference was made at the
end of the last chapter to the way in which the artist helps
us to *see as*. In the great Resurrection scene, painted by the
English artist Stanley Spencer in the memorial chapel at
Burghclere, all the soldiers who are rising from the dead give
their crosses to Christ; but only the artist himself, gazing

contemplatively at the crucifix, sees the true significance of what is happening. As we share in the Eucharist we find that through sharing this bread, taking it physically into our bodies, we can begin to understand and live the truth that God is incarnate for and in us.

• *in the same way with the cup after supper, saying 'This cup is the new covenant in my blood'*
The significance of all things, 'the love that moves the sun and the other stars',[4] is not clean and aseptic. It is passionate, suffering, absolute love. Through drinking of this cup (if we dare) we enter into new relationship with God, not based on bargains and laws, but alive with all the risks and dynamism of divine love.

• *Do this in remembrance of me*
In these actions we call to mind the essence of what Christ is to us and we to Christ. What is important is to do what the disciples were doing then, namely receiving from God and sharing between themselves. There is no suggestion that one special disciple, or even all the disciples, should take the part of Jesus Christ in this drama. They are to remember what Christ has done, and will continue to do, in and for them.

• *Whenever you eat this bread and drink this cup you are proclaiming the Lord's death until he comes*
1. Through repeatedly re-enacting this event we keep alive the true nature of Christ throughout subsequent history
2. By being broken in love ourselves, we re-present the sacrificial death of Christ to the world
3. We are assured that the Christ will come again and that we have a part to play in the waiting and preparation.

The depth of the mystery of the Eucharist is rooted in its ordinariness. Ordinary bread and wine, our lives as they are, remain as they are, yet are truly the body and blood of Christ. Jesus Christ, the Word of God, the meaning of all that has been, is and will be, becomes part of our life experience. We, as the community that shares in this bread, become the body of Christ: the very bread that is broken. The Eucharist therefore grows out of normal everyday life and experience and is essentially a community activity.

It was this rootedness in reality that gave such dynamism to the early Christians who met to re-enact that event, and that has in recent years empowered the poor of Latin America through the development of base ecclesial communities. Deep down the faithful have clung on to this truth, not always able to articulate it but knowing that through it their lives have been transformed; and this faith, this truth and this reality have sustained the Church through centuries in which the basic actions have gathered many good and bad accretions.

Those who gather for the Eucharist *are* the body of Christ, and in the same way as James encourages the early Christians to confess their sins to each other rather than going to a priest; so the body of Christ has no need of an intermediary to unwrap for them the deep religious significance of life through re-enactment of the Last Supper.

This ultimate sacrament, this truth beneath all truths and this life-giving embodiment of God, is complete in itself and cannot require another sacrament (ordination) to render it effective. The Eucharist is therefore a sacrament regardless of whether it is presided over by an ordained priest; and where such an ordained priest, or anyone else, is fulfilling a priestly role at communion this has more to do with the trust invested in that person by the congregation (for whatever reason) than with the conferring of a special and permanent status on them at a formal initiation ceremony called ordination.[5]

Restoring Eucharist to the priesthood of all believers

We have noted that reforming movements in the Church have nearly always allowed themselves, immediately or eventually, to be deprived of the sacraments. Is it possible, now, for those who long to release the power of the sacraments in the Church by restoring the Eucharist to the common priesthood, to refuse to be ousted? Prophets are in general made as uncomfortable in the Church as they were in the Jewish religion; but through the grace and discomforting power of the Holy Spirit they are sometimes constrained and enabled to outstay their welcome. The Eucharist belongs to all Christian people, and no one on earth, of whatever rank or hierarchy, has the right to cheat the faithful of this life-giving sacrament.

The idea of lay celebration is enough to give many clergy apoplexy; but what do such clergy fear will happen if lay people 'do it themselves'? If they believe that it is not a sacrament without the good offices of an ordained priest, and that the significance is not released, there is nothing to worry about. If it is clearly not going to work, then it might be considered something of a waste of time, but can hardly be said to hurt anyone. If people want to take part in an activity similar to one that normally occurs within the context (and confines) of the Church then that is no one's business but their own. We do not object when we see children playing doctors and nurses with their friends and dispensing clean water on a teaspoon.

If on the other hand the sacrament *is* valid, and what the people are doing is recognisably and effectually the same as that which through the ages has taken place in a church and been presided over by an ordained person, then what on earth is anyone trying to do by discouraging this activity? What sense can we give to our responsibility to bring in the reign of God, gathering all people into the love and knowledge of God?

Most people, certainly most Christians, would far rather conform and obey than challenge and resist authority. It would appear, however, that a Church inspired by the Holy Spirit must be dynamic, and that the symbol of a pilgrim people is more appropriate than that of Lot's wife petrified in salt (Gen. 19:26). In the same way as many in the churches appear to have been led by the Holy Spirit to break the laws about communion between certain denominations, so it is undeniable that many Eucharists are now celebrated without the presence of an ordained priest; and the lack of sanction by the Church appears to make no difference at all to the efficacy and importance of the sacrament to those taking part, many of whom discover, through the liberation

afforded in these situations, a release of the power of the
Holy Spirit in their lives.

However, if anyone and everyone could celebrate the
Eucharist, with no constraints or safeguards, we should risk
losing the sense of what this sacrament is. The Eucharist
may not need an ordained priesthood, but like any other
sacrament it does need to be regulated by the Church. The
fact that orders are not a necessary part of our sacramental
life does not mean that we can dispense with *order*. The
Eucharist is a *communal* act by the Church and, contrary to
the non-ecumenical appearances that generally pertain, the
whole Church should be fully represented in each celebration of the Eucharist. Leaving aside, for the moment, the
sense many such groups have that they are being driven to
holy disobedience by the Holy Spirit, how can groups of
people who consciously break the present laws of the Church
be said to represent that Church and to be doing something
consistent with and on behalf of the Church universal?

Rather than answering that question in abstract terms, I
choose to describe a group with which I have been closely
connected for over twenty years: to share the way that group
grappled with the centrality of the Eucharist and tackled the
ordination problem, describe some of the fruits by which
the group has been known, and explore some of the possible
implications for the 'great Church'.

One community's journey to full priesthood

The group was formed in pain, at a time when the church
that most of its members attended was failing to offer teaching, example or pastoral support. A number of deeply committed people, from a wide age range, were drawn together:
some of them could possibly be classed as 'discontents' by
the Church, but others were obedient members of the congregation who would never have dreamed of being involved
in subversion in any form. Most, though not all, were Christians; most, though not all, were fairly educated and articulate. Most denominations were represented, and for one

married couple in which the husband was Protestant and the wife Roman Catholic, it was the only situation in which they were able to take communion together as their Roman Catholic bishop had forbidden intercommunion.

The group met once a month to discuss, to pray and to explore ways in which they could all take part in worship rather than being spoon-fed at every service. Some members of the group were clergy, so there was no problem in celebrating the Eucharist, which became the heart of the group's activity around which everything else revolved. Here was a safe forum in which those to whom such things mattered could experiment with the liturgy and increase their involvement.

A form of service evolved: moving round the circle, different people read the various parts of the service, while at the absolution, consecration and blessing, the whole group, as the body of Christ, said the words together. As there was generally at least one ordained member present, no rules were, strictly, being broken, as that person's presence (crazily) validated the sacrament. As an experiment it was working, though obviously by seeking validity through one person's presence we were implicitly diminishing the role of all the other members.

A number of senior church people visited the group, to lead discussion on particular issues, but also to share in the life of the group. It was a visiting bishop who first challenged us to rethink our position of being dependent on the ordained members. What, he asked, would we do when, as was at some point inevitable, there was no ordained person present? Did we cease to function as the Church and deprive each other of the very sacrament that was sustaining us in our lives and in our local church situation? With his help and encouragement, and with much heart-searching among the group (this was in the 1970s, not the 1990s!), the decision was made that with or without ordained people present, the sacrifice went on, the sacrament was to be celebrated. Immediately we found the nature of the service changed, as everyone realised that it was they, not the person in the corner who had left his dog collar at home, who were validating this holy sacrament.

No one left when this decision was made, and everyone appeared to find it a valuable departure. But two groups of people in particular were enthusiastic about the change. Women expressed their wonderment that they (who at this point could not be ordained in the Anglican Church) could say these words; and pointed out how much more powerful the same words now became when they heard them said at their normal church service on Sunday. The other group were the clergy members, who discovered that for the first time they were liberated to be part of the body of Christ, rather than always having to be and do something special for the sake of everyone else. The words took on new significance and power for them as they were, at last, fully admitted as part of the body of Christ rather than as a (favourite) appendage.

In line with ancient Christian tradition, a period of persecution by the Church ensued, with perjuries committed by odd members of the church hierarchy who did not know, and appeared not to want to know, what went on at the housegroup services, but were fairly sure it should not be happening. This persecution culminated in an honest and amicable talk with the local Anglican bishop, who had the percipience to realise that what was going on, though it could be claimed to infringe certain rules, was a good and holy thing. As so often in the Church, the charge he laid on the group at this stage was to keep quiet about what we were doing, but get on with it.

Sharing and growth continued, and in time another prophet came to us, in the person of Alan Ecclestone, one of the greatest figures of the Anglican Church in the twentieth century. Having shared his wisdom and wit with us and treated us to some of his amazing store of learning and love of literature, he challenged us over the way we were keeping our heads down and getting on with what we wanted to do without rocking the boat too much in the wider Church. He talked at length about the riches we had been given as the small Church, and our subsequent responsibility to share

those and feed them back into the great Church. Our diplo-
macy and concern not to offend, which had allowed us to
get on with what we were doing without further persecution,
began to smack slightly of cowardice; and he suggested to
us in no uncertain terms that it was our duty to the Church
to 'come out' and face the music, so that what we had
received could begin to exercise an influence on the whole
institution.

Although there is still a good deal of ignorance over what
actually happens at our meetings, the local hierarchy now
accept us to such an extent that we are in danger of becoming
'respectable', which may possibly represent a greater risk in
the long term than the persecution we had to suffer many
years ago. Very little of any moment happens in the local
church without the involvement, and in almost every case,
the leadership of the members of the housegroup. The continued freedom to experiment has given rise to a continually
evolving form of Eucharist and the group, which remains
open to any whose needs it is likely to meet, responds to the
ideas of its members as they arise. Above all, the members
of the housegroup offer care and support to each other, and
travel with each other spiritually and emotionally, sharing
doubts and insecurities as well as intellectual suggestions
and insights.

The experience of this group is offered, not as a template
for success, for the group is not without its difficulties and
frustrations; but as the real story of how one group of
ordinary people responded to their particular situation and
were led through various difficulties to be the Church. None
of the members of that group were seeking ordained priesthood, but through the grace of God all have begun to explore
and understand what their common priesthood might mean.

Such groups are not, however, alternatives to the Church;
they are complementary to it. The more we are fed and
encouraged by the small Church in action, the more responsibility we have to share what we have gained and to be
prepared to be involved in forcing change from below.
Cliques, as the Taizé community wisely realised very early
in its life, are no use to anyone. Despite appearances and

the impatience of those caught up in the grinding machinery of institutional religion, the Church does respond to pressure from the grass roots. Only by engaging deeply with the great Church, staying in full, loving, defiant relationship, can the gifts that the Holy Spirit is pouring on small groups effect change for all who need it.

In the context of the freedom of the whole people of God to exercise the full priesthood conferred on them at baptism, we can now look at the final sacrament, namely the sacrament of ordination.

11

Ordination

In looking at the various sacraments it has become clear that there is nothing in matrimony, baptism, confirmation, penance, anointing or holy communion for which ordination is truly essential. We come now to the sacrament of Orders itself and must attempt to apply the same sort of analysis as we did in the case of the other sacraments. What exactly is the sacrament of ordination?

Our starting point must be the recognition that ordination has not traditionally been considered to be a major sacrament. We saw in chapter 9 that it is not included among the major sacraments of either the Roman Catholic or Anglican Churches. The Anglican Book of Common Prayer specifically states that ordination is of a lower order than holy communion and baptism. The drafting of Article XXV was rather less generous to the Roman Catholic Church than might have been desirable, but the distinction between two levels of sacraments is clear:

> There are two Sacraments ordained of Christ our Lord in the Gospel, that is to say, Baptism, and the Supper of the Lord.
>
> Those five commonly called Sacraments, that is to say, Confirmation, Penance, Orders, Matrimony, and extreme Unction, are not to be counted for Sacraments of the Gospel, being such as have grown partly of the corrupt following of the Apostles, partly are states of life allowed in the Scriptures; but yet have not like nature of Sacraments with Baptism, and the Lord's Supper, for that they have not any visible sign or ceremony ordained of God.

The Roman Catholic Church, too, however, would distinguish between those sacraments that are founded in Scripture and those that are not.

As a greater sacrament (holy communion) cannot require a lesser sacrament (ordination) to validate it, we have concluded that the validity of the sacrament of holy communion cannot be dependent on whether or not the celebrant is ordained. Conversely, if there *is* a sacrament of Orders, then the sacramental validity must come from the ordination itself, not from participation in another sacrament. The fact that someone is licensed to celebrate holy communion does not in itself make that person a priest. If they are to have any force or value, the sacraments of both holy communion and ordination should be perceived as complete and valid in themselves.

The service of ordination

It may be a result of ordination falling within this 'second division' of sacraments, or it may be one of the causes of that demotion; but it must be admitted that the service of ordination lacks much of the richness of action and symbol that enlivens other major sacraments. This is not to deny that the ordination service can be both meaningful and deeply moving to those who participate in it; but if the service is analysed it will be found that it contains little that would distinguish it from a commissioning ceremony for any other profession or task.

G. K. Chesteron's indictment of Christianity as 'poor talkative little Christianity' has all too familiar a ring in describing much that goes on in the Church, but it is by no means the whole story. Quite apart from the fact that there is a long tradition of silence and stillness in the Christian Church that for countless of the faithful represents the kernel of their spiritual life, there is also a recognition, in many of the Christian traditions, of the power of symbol and sacrament. For this reason, when we attempt to express truths that are too deep for words we often find we need to have recourse to sacraments, in which words are superseded or rendered unnecessary. It is by thus leaping over the limitations of words that sacraments can achieve power beyond what human beings can understand or express.

Some of the sacraments are particularly rich in symbolism and non-verbal communication. For instance in *baptism*, water is used, the sign of the cross is imprinted on the flesh, light is given in the form of a candle, and sometimes a garment is donned as well. Each of these actions and gifts resonates deeply and expresses far more than could any bald statements about what it is to be a member of the Church. Similarly, at the wedding which marks the outset of *marriage*, rings are exchanged, hands are held, legal changes in family allegiance are effected, there is a dance in which those who arrive at the church separately leave as a couple. In *anointing* there is the use of oil, and the physical action of the laying on of hands. In *holy communion* not only are the bread and wine more evocative than almost any other symbols used by human beings, and take on added potency by becoming physically part of our bodies, but there are also other important symbolic actions such as greeting other people in the Peace, moving physically to the altar and being sent out in the power of the Spirit.

In contrast to these rich sacraments, penance, confirmation and orders appear a little tame and undeveloped. *Penance* cries out for sacramental actions, such as burning paper, leaving a stone, washing oneself, or holding the hand of the person who has been wronged. Actions such as these can be explored within communities and groups, and will generally lead to a deepening of the sacramental nature of the service but they are not, as yet, understood to be essential parts of the sacrament, which resides almost exclusively in the exchange of words.

In both *confirmation* and *ordination*, the bishop's hands are laid on the head of the candidate, and this action draws power from the authority vested in the bishop by the whole Church. However, the fact that the same action by the same authority takes place at the two sacraments might cause one to wonder if there is any substantial difference between confirmation and ordination. Apart from the adoption of a different set of words, the only obvious difference is that the new priest is then given a Bible (or in the case of deacons, a New Testament) as a symbol of their new commission to expound the faith. Some of the vigour has gone out of the choice of this gift: partly because Bibles are now so common in developed countries that it is highly unlikely that the priest will have any real need for an additional such book; and partly because many other people expound Scripture and teach the faithful besides the priest, so that it is questionable what the priest is here being empowered to do.

If we can come to a clearer understanding of the nature of ordination and its relationship with priesthood, it may well be that we shall be able to express that more meaningfully in word and action, and initiation into ordained priesthood will become richer.

Empowerment through ordination

In ancient times, priests were thought to receive special power from God; and they were also invested with power by the people who recognized their priesthood. This association of priesthood and power still operates in the Church's understanding and practice, even in those denominations that refer to their ordained members as ministers.

A critical issue in the theology of priesthood concerns the empowerment that is associated with it. Western theology, whether one accepts or rejects the mediaeval understanding of priesthood, has viewed ordination as the conferral of power by Christ, specifically, the power to consecrate, to offer sacrifice and to forgive sin. What needs to be recovered is the fact that Christ's own priesthood is given him by the Father through the consecration of the Spirit. So it is also with all manifestations of Christ's priesthood. The power of priesthood, whether of the church, of the baptized, or of the ministerial priesthood, is not possessed, but trusted. The invocations of both baptism and ordination are acts of entrustment whereby individuals are placed at the disposal of God's Spirit, and their lives and ministries entrusted to the Spirit's care. Any image of either baptism or ordination which sees the power of priesthood possessed by individuals, or even by the church, seriously distorts the reality of the Holy Spirit who is the source of all Christian priesthood.[1]

One of the ways in which clergy power is manifested is in their exclusive right to celebrate the Eucharist. This was not always the case, for until the fourth century bishops were the only ones who celebrated the sacraments, and priests (presbyters) were commissioned workers. In the fourth century this changed, as celebrating the Eucharist became the prerogative of the ordained priests. Instead of commissioning workers to action, ordination began to confer power; and in time, unfortunately, the corollary of this empowerment of the clergy was the disempowerment of the rest of the Church.

Instead of being the means by which the power of the sacraments is released into the world, ordination has sometimes effectively come to represent that which separates people from the sacraments. As a result, those who are ordained as priests have found themselves exercising control over the people of God and holding a monopoly of the sacred. Any system that starts from a position of disempowering the people of God and disallowing the sacraments must diminish, rather than build up, the Church and her mission in the world.

Locus of sacrament

There is the same confusion over ordination as there was over marriage and weddings. Is it *priesthood* that is meant to be the sacrament, or *ordination*? In other words, is the sacrament the service at which someone is commissioned to work in the Church as an ordained person, or is the sacrament the state of being in some sense a 'special' person from that time on? The answer to this question will have implications for the discussion of whether the ordained ministry is functional or ontological that was raised in chapter 8.

The question was raised, in chapter 8, as to whether those who are ordained are priests while performing certain actions such as baptism and consecrating the elements at holy communion; or all the time, while enjoying a drink with friends, changing their children's nappies or driving down the motorway? If the sacrament of priesthood is concentrated into certain particular holy moments, then does it matter who or what the celebrant is for the rest of the time? If it is all the time, then why is it that there are and always have been ordained priests who are clearly not in a state of grace and who in their everyday lives do little to reflect the glory and love of God?

The Christian Church has always maintained that a communicant can receive sacramental grace despite the unworthiness of the priest who officiates at the service. Conversely, participation in a sacrament, be it Eucharist or Ordination, does not by and in itself ensure that sacramental grace is received. Many clergy have been constrained by circumstances to go on celebrating the Eucharist when the words and actions seemed dead, their souls were in torment, or even, *in extremis*, they had ceased to believe in God. It is possible, too, for those receiving communion to do it through force of habit or in a state of spiritual torment or isolation in which light cannot pierce the darkness.

Throughout history there have been people who have been ordained for opportunistic reasons, or because their family demanded that a particular son should enter the Church, or because they were no good at anything else. Are we really committed to believing that a one-off event of ordination necessarily makes these people into priests? When it comes to opening to others the mystery and power of the Eucharist, does it make any sense at all to claim that being in a state of sin does not matter, but being ordained does?

Marriage and baptism are considered to be 'one-off' sacraments, only repeated in exceptional circumstances and by bending either the rules or the logic. Once married or baptised, one is married or baptised all the time, not just while in bed with one's spouse, or taking part in activities at church. Other sacraments are repeatable: for example, for most of us it would take far more than a lifetime of partaking of the Eucharist to embody that sacrament fully in our life and soul. Although the effect of holy communion, confession or anointing may continue long after the sacramental action has been concluded, the sacrament itself finishes with the close of the service. On which side of this line does ordination fall? Is it unique like baptism, confirmation and marriage, or repeatable like Eucharist, confession and anointing?

This distinction, however, is not as clear cut as at first appears. If I confess a sin and know myself to be absolved, I cannot then need to confess that sin and be absolved again. I may commit other sins, and need to address those, but that particular sin is forgiven for ever. The sacrament is as unique as baptism. We may feel that we later lose the state of grace we attained when attending communion, but if the sacrament is valid we can never go back on that particular experience of meeting and identifying with God through Jesus Christ. One confession or one experience of participating in the Eucharist can change someone's life for ever, and conversely it is possible for a baptism or a marriage to change nothing.

The 'unique' sacraments are no more powerful than the repeatable ones and need to be worked on and renewed continually in order to remain sacramental. Instead of seeing baptism as a one-off event, perhaps we should recognise that it only makes sense to speak of being 'born again' if we see that as a continuous, or at least an oft-repeated, activity. Such an approach would also explain why those who have married with the best of intentions, and attempted to live out the sacrament of marriage, can find, if the relationship is not fed and renewed, that the marriage has died. As we saw in chapter 9, it is not the event on the wedding day that makes it a sacrament, but the estate in which the couple then live. The event marks and celebrates the sacrament in which they partake, and commits them to a certain life thereafter.

In the case of all the sacraments there is the 'now' and the 'always'. Something can hardly be expected to count as a sacrament if participation in that event makes no difference to the person, even in the short term. A sacrament comprises a combination of certain actions and words now, and certain states or understandings that continue.

However, even with the sacraments that are repeated, there is a long-term as well as a short-term effect. In looking at the temporal location of sacraments, it is possible to mark a threefold progression. Each sacrament

a) reflects an already existing reality
b) symbolically marks a point in sacred time
c) changes something for the future

Each of these stages can be publicly verified in some way, and b) is generally a public event.

In *marriage*, for example, a) is love and the establishment of the prime pairing bond; b) is the wedding, which is a public affirmation; and c) is the whole future of commitment and total sharing, including the full expression and celebration of sexual love. *Baptism*, in its pure form, follows the same pattern, with a) belief in and desire to follow Jesus Christ; b) symbolic cleansing from sin and rebirth into the community of Christians; and c) the responsibilities and privileges of being part of the royal priesthood. Again, in *absolution*, we have a) the recognition of sin and intention to relinquish it; b) a public admission of fault, expression of regret and acceptance of God's forgiveness; c) freedom from guilt and grace to live better. The public nature of the sacrament of absolution applies even if only one other person is involved.

If this three-fold progression is the common pattern for sacraments, how does, or should, it work with ordination? Exactly the same pattern should apply, with a) recognition by the Christian community, rather than a centralized ecclesial body from outside, that this person is representative of their priesthood; b) a public acceptance of that position, in which the person takes full responsibility and is commissioned to fulfil a certain function; and c) there should follow a life in which living and sharing priesthood is at the top of the priest's priorities. The service of ordination is as important as a wedding service to all involved because it marks and celebrates priesthood: it does not create it.

We saw that in marriage the true sacrament is in the continuing life lived by the couple, rather than the symbolic words and gestures that occur on their wedding day. If we were to look for a parallel with the ordained priesthood, we would expect to find that the *sacrament* is priesthood, not just the ordination service; and priesthood, of course, is for all Christians. On this interpretation, ordination is simply the public acceptance and recognition of the sacrament of priesthood. The difficulty with this approach, however, is that we already have a sacrament that initiates us into priesthood, namely baptism. What is the purpose of ordination that differentiates it from baptism?

Ministry and priesthood

If ordination is simply a commissioning by the Church to do a certain job, like the appointment of a church warden or chorister, then it is difficult to interpret this event in terms of a sacrament. There is no reason why a commissioning service may not be beautiful and moving, and it can certainly be a significant and important ceremony within the Church, but that does not make it a sacrament. If, on the other hand, ordination is intimately connected with priesthood, then it is relevant to ask if baptismal priesthood is any less of a sacrament than ordained priesthood.

It will be argued in the next chapter that the true sacrament is the priesthood of all believers, because the priestly life of the faithful reveals to us the nature of Christ's priesthood. If ordination is understood within that context, then it is appropriate to ordain those who are recognised by the Christian community as exemplifying priesthood, to represent them in their priestly vocation. Ordination would thus become not only a public affirmation and celebration of the priestly nature of the candidate, but a distillation and a symbol of true priesthood.

A symbol is not the same thing as a sacrament. In marriage, for example, the ring is a symbol of eternal love and the joining of hands is symbolic of the new identity of this couple in the eyes of the world; while sexual intercourse, or the creation and nurturing of new life, or the pattern of reconciliation after conflict, and loyalty in time of testing are sacramental, for they draw aside the veil to show us more of the nature of God. Ordination can, and should, be a powerful symbol of the priesthood that we all share.

The purpose of the sacrament is to reveal and recognise, not to create. In the same way that the wedding service does not make people love each other, but is indicative of an experienced reality and a commitment to experience the love of God in their life together, so ordination will not make anyone a priest. In so far as ordination contributes to the priesthood of all believers, however, and draws its meaning and potency from that understanding of Christian priesthood, it has an important part to play in the sacrament of priesthood.

In assessing the nature of priesthood, therefore, it is vital to differentiate clearly between baptismal priesthood and ordained priesthood. Both may be equally valuable, and there should certainly be no hierarchy of functions within the Church, as is spelled out quite clearly in 1 Corinthians 12.

However, rather than defining baptismal priesthood by reference to or by extrapolating from the ordained priesthood, we should be defining ordained priesthood by reference to the priesthood of all believers. If we can be clear about what this *priesthood* is, then we might become clearer about the importance and function of ordination. It is to this sacrament of the priesthood of all believers that we turn in the next chapter.

12

The nature of priesthood for all Christians

The concept of 'priesthood', which arises from deep within the consciousness and history of the human race, reverberates with powerful imagery and is too vital to be appropriated by the career structures of a few denominations or even confined to one religion. Is it possible to reinstate it at the centre of our religious experience?

We have seen that one of the revolutionary innovations of the movement begun by Jesus Christ was that all were called to a new form of priesthood. Any old religion can have priests; this movement offered something rather different by calling people to put aside the old order and enter into new life in God. But what is it that we are called to be and to do?

Given that the only references to Christian priesthood in the New Testament relate either to Christ himself or to all Christian people, we should attempt to understand the latter in the light of the former. The word 'priest' is used so rarely in the New Testament that we may assume that there was good reason for the writer of the First Epistle of Peter, when describing the Christian vocation, and the writer of the Revelation to St John (1:6, 5:9–10; 20:6), in referring to the community of the faithful, to choose the same word as the writer of Hebrews chose to expound the salvific work of Christ.

We speak of Jesus Christ as our 'great high priest'. Our priesthood is a sacrament because and in so far as it reveals to us the nature of Christ's priesthood. Through Christ's priesthood we learn what priesthood is meant to be; and if we are to use the same concept of priesthood to apply to ourselves, it is clear that our priesthood must be modelled on him. The priesthood of Christ, the incarnate God, was revealed in a life of humility, service, truth, vulnerability and love; which suggests that these must be the essential characteristics that should define priesthood for us too.

The functions of priesthood

But besides these qualities, to which all Christians are called to aspire, are there *functions* of priesthood exemplified in Jesus Christ that are applicable to us in our own exercise of priesthood? Two such functions stand out clearly, particularly in the interpretation of Christ's priesthood that is worked out in the Letter to the Hebrews.

First, Jesus the Christ *presents God to the world and the world to God* (6:19–20; 7:25; 8:1). The incarnation achieves this supremely; but it is what we are all required to do in our varying ways. We are not called to be intermediaries, for nothing should come between God and humanity. We are called to be bridges; and it is significant that the word 'pontiff' was chosen by the popes to describe what, at their best, they aspired to be.

We are all called to live out the incarnation in the world now, breaking down the artificial barrier between the sacred and the secular. Any organisation that hives people off from the world into a separate religious caste has missed the point of the incarnation. *This* is the world that God has created, loved and redeemed. This is where we live Christ's presence in the world. Only if we are revealing God to those around us are we exercising our priesthood; and this applies to ordained and lay alike.

The second feature of priesthood we see in Jesus Christ is the ancient function of *offering sacrifice*: the role played by priests in many religions (Heb. 7:27). As far as we know, Jesus Christ did not perform any sacrificial rites at all, but he lived a life that was worthy to be offered to God, and it was one that was wholly characterised by self-sacrifice; even to the extent of offering the ultimate sacrifice of his own life (Heb. 9:12, 14, 28).

So priests after the Order of Jesus Christ (rather, perhaps, than after the order of Melchizedek) are those who truly serve God with all their heart and soul: not counting the cost or furthering their careers, but offering to God their worship, love and gratitude; all that they do and are and hope for. They are the ones who are prepared to live self-sacrificially, who love to the death, who are prepared to lose life to save it. The human race has been privileged to have priests like this since time immemorial. Such priests form a triumphant priestly procession throughout history, and are as much in evidence today as ever.

If we use our imaginations we will recognize faces in that procession. Yes, Mother Teresa, Steve Biko and Mahatma Ghandi might well be there, along with other examples of the great and the good; but if we look carefully we shall also recognise priests who have not caught the world's eye, but who have daily and hourly offered the sacrifice most pleasing to God. They come from all countries, creeds and classes, and do not in general capture the news headlines. We might see the grandparents who skimp, and save to give everything they have, in order to make life better for a braindamaged grandchild; the woman who gives up her career to look after a sick relative; the Greenpeace volunteers who take ghastly risks to raise our consciousness of the evil perpetrated on the environment in our name; the employer who, confronted with equal candidates for a job chooses to give employment to the black applicant, or the one with a physical handicap; the refugee who gives his blanket to a child.

But over and above all these individuals in whom we see clear marks of priesthood, is the priesthood that we exercise corporately because we are the Church, the community of all the baptised. In so far as the Church is the body of Christ on earth, it will bear within itself the marks of suffering love. In response to human needs the Church has often been presented as a powerful, wealthy fortress to protect its own from the exigencies of life. That is why we have inherited some strange concepts of priesthood that do not and cannot feed the faithful or save the world. The body of Christ is always and essentially broken and crucified in love: therein lies the only hope of resurrection.

Readiness to face suffering if necessary has a long history in the Christian Church; and in the Revelation to St John we read that those who have been martyred for Christ 'will be priests of God and of Christ and reign with him for a thousand years' (20:6). Similarly, when St Paul needs to present his credentials for writing to the young churches, he does so in terms of the sufferings he has endured, rather than any superior theological training, apostolic commissioning or status; and it is as one undergoing suffering that he is able to write to urge others to live up to the ideal of Christian priesthood: 'I, the prisoner in the Lord, urge you therefore to lead a life worthy of the vocation to which you were called' (Eph. 4:1). This is the ideal; not power or knowledge or birth. This is how Paul understands Jesus' radical reinterpretation of priesthood.

There is nothing in all this about special privileges, or leadership skills, or bearing responsibility for running the local church. It is offering sacrifices that makes people priests. What is more, it is the royal way of Jesus Christ, to which we are all called.

Make your own mind the mind of Christ:
Who, being in the form of God,
did not count equality with God
something to be grasped,
But emptied himself,
taking the form of a slave,
becoming as human beings are;
and being in every way like a human being,
he was humbler yet,
even to accepting death, death on a cross. (Phil. 2:6–8)

So if Christ is our high priest because he sacrifices himself, we too are called to be priests by living that same self-sacrificial love. It is unnerving to realise that this may be one of the reasons that Peter recognises all Christians as having a vocation to priesthood.

The uncomfortable truth of Christianity is that if we respond to the call to follow Christ we become part of the body of Christ and enter thereby into priesthood. To accept and begin to learn how to exercise our priesthood is not to abrogate to ourselves the status and privilege that have so often led astray the ordained all down the corridors of history, but to humbly and faithfully offer sacrifice to God; for suffering self-sacrifice is a far clearer indicator of priesthood than ordination.

> Only as the Church lets itself be implicated in Christ's death and in His reproach, can it minister in His ministry. Only as it learns to let the mind of Christ be in its mind, and is inwardly and outwardly shaped by His servant-obedience unto the death of the Cross, can it participate in His Prophetic, Priestly, and Kingly Ministry . . . Not by standing on its dignity, or vaunting its rights, not by lordly rule or patronage, not by any wielding of worldly authority and glory, can the Church effectively fulfil its ministry, but by renouncing all these as the temptation of Satan. It is when the Church is ready to be made of no reputation that it is ready to participate in Christ's own ministry.[1]

Jesus warned of the nature of Christian priesthood even before the Passion. When James and John ask if they can be next to him in his glory (sit in full view of the congregation, process in to church wearing fine robes, lay down the law about what goes on in the services), Jesus returns an unexpected backhand and assures them that it is indeed going to be their privilege to share his baptism and his cup: to give themselves to God and to accept suffering and self-sacrifice; but that this has nothing to do with privilege or status (Mark 10:41–5; Luke 22:24–7). To read into this conversation between Jesus and the two brothers any hint of priestly instruction would be far-fetched and non-contextual; but it is interesting that the model James and John are given relates closely to the model of priesthood that we have found in Jesus Christ.

There are, therefore, two functions of true priesthood that

we, in embracing our own priesthood as Christians, should seek to emulate as we take as our pattern of priesthood the person of Jesus Christ.

• We are to seek, in all we are and do, to present God to the world and the world to God (sharing Christ's baptism)
• We are to live lives of self-sacrificing love (sharing his cup)

Throughout history priests in many cultures and religions have offered sacrifice. But as Jesus's contemporaries already knew from reciting Psalm 51, 'The sacrifice of God is a broken spirit' and Isaiah, Hosea and others had long ago drummed home the message that God is not interested in slain animals but in human beings living in holy, sacrificial ways. As early as Deuteronomy there was a clear grasp that the sacrifice required of God had more to do with lifestyle than blood-letting: 'What doth the Lord require of thee, but to fear the Lord thy God, to walk in all his ways, and to love him and to serve him with all thy heart and all thy soul (10:12).

In the ancient traditions of priesthood, the priest was bound to offer only the best to God. No animal could be offered unless it was perfect and unblemished. Part of presenting God to the world and the world to God is to reveal the perfect goodness of God, and to present in gratitude the best that the world can offer.

So it is that, although Christian priesthood embraces suffering, it is also essentially about gratitude and joy, as we offer back to God the best of our lives. All that is pure and holy, beautiful and true is part of our daily offering to God, freely given in delight at all we have received. This is what worship is, and why at those times when we have some experience of living close to God, prayer bubbles out of us as part of our loving response. 'Through him, let us offer God an unending sacrifice of praise, the fruit of the lips of those who acknowledge his name. Keep doing good works and sharing your resources, for these are the kinds of sacrifice that please God' (Heb. 13:15–16).

All are called

To put all this in more mundane terms: Jesus called people
to a life, a 'kingdom', not a Church. What matters, in winning the world for Christ, is that people should live a certain
sort of life whether or not they are baptised, or take communion. Similarly all are called to live priestly lives, irrespec-
tive of whether those lives are marked by ordination.

'Lay' is far too often used to suggest that someone is just
an amateur who is not qualified for something. Yet there is
no higher recommendation or qualification for life or for
priesthood than to be part of the *laos*, the people of God,
the chosen race.

The laity, just as much as the ordained, are called to lead
and be the Church; and part of that leading and being is to
make the sacraments available. This is not a role that is
subsidiary to the ordained priesthood, but that works in
true partnership with it. Douglas Rhymes wrote in *Layman's
Church*, not now in the present intellectual climate but in
1963:

> The laity must then take their rightful place of leadership
> with and not below the clergy; claiming the right to initiate
> action, to decide for themselves what is the best form of
> service and not to be immersed in a host of organizations
> just because that is what the clergy conceive as working
> for the Church, seeking themselves to teach and be taught,
> working out with the clergy what is the best way to inte-
> grate faith to life and worship to life. It is a partnership of
> equals in which each has his own peculiar function but in
> which both are working as partners in a common concern
> – the redemption of the world, and working as common
> members of the whole people of God, the laos to which
> both clergy and laity belong.[2]

Sacraments, too, can be efficacious without the presence
of an ordained priest. Many people in the Church believe
that only a priest can absolve from sin or bless; yet friends
and lovers frequently absolve each other by and through
their love, and blessing is the prerogative of all Christian

people. Countless parents bless their children, and it is not unknown for children to reciprocate by blessing them. More generally, we all know what it is to be blessed by contact with a person of God, and these people are more likely to be humbly living in the spirit of the beatitudes than passing examinations in theology or drawing a stipend from the Church. The colloquial 'bless you' many not have all the force of its original meaning, but for better or worse it is part of our common currency, and arguably still carries the essence of real blessing.

None of these concepts of blessing has anything to do with ordination, except in so far as ordination bestows on a priest the charge to tell people that they are blessed. But as in other duties of the ordained priest, that is also the duty of all within the priesthood of all believers. Our priesthood is pretty worthless if it does not bring blessing to those with whom we come into contact.

The corporate nature of priesthood

The priesthood of all believers, however, does not define a collection of individuals who are priests. In the New Testament the term is used only in the plural, to denote our collective priesthood, and it describes the people who belong to the body of Christ which is the Church. This is consistent with the earliest understanding of the Jewish nation as a kingdom of priests (see chapter 3), and can be seen as a return to a purer understanding of priesthood.

In the same way, in the early Church it was the whole community that was apostolic. Any special duties that fell to 'the twelve' came to them by virtue of their membership of that group, representing all of humanity by reference to the twelve tribes of Israel, not as individuals. The priesthood of all the baptised, to which Peter refers, arises simply and solely from membership of the community.

It is vital that we should understand our priesthood corporately rather than individually. 'Priests' and 'kings' are words that apply to us all as the body of Christ. That does not mean that I am a priest, or you are a king. It means that together we have a role to play in the world which is authoritative and sacerdotal. A strong doctrine of the priesthood of all believers maintains this corporate understanding of our priesthood far more effectively than ordination to the priesthood does. Christianity is ultimately about community, not privilege or individualism. The fact that it is *all* believers, not every believer, who carry priesthood means that ordained priests have no special right to the term. They, like other Christians, draw their priesthood from their membership of the royal priesthood of all believers. All are chosen.

The word 'saints' is another plural word that is always used collectively in the New Testament, and the fact that we are part of the household of saints, called to live out a holy life, does not mean that any one of us necessarily qualifies to have the denotation 'Saint' prefixed to our name. The same applies to the *laos*. It means the people, not the person, of God. We all share this privilege, and it is high time that the laity welcomed the ordained into their community. While it is true that ordination has disabled the laity from performing many of the priestly tasks that are their duty and prerogative, it is also true that the laity has disabled the clergy by excluding them from truly being members of the Christian community. The gospel that Jesus Christ offered was not a private, individualistic religion, but a new and life-enhancing way of being community.

All are called to life in God, and acceptance of the gospel is an individual act: no one can do it for us. But once we accept Jesus Christ into our lives, we become part of the new creation, just as much as those who 'have done a heavy day's work in all the heat' (Matt. 20:12). There is no question of some of the latecomers gleaning the crumbs dropped by a higher order, for all are a holy people, part of the Temple. 'So you are no longer aliens or foreign visitors; you are fellow-citizens with the holy people of God and part of God's household. You are built upon the foundation of the apostles and prophets, and Christ Jesus is the corner-stone' (Eph. 2:19).

We have seen how over the years a totally artificial distinction between clergy and laity has developed in the Church. New Testament Christians knew that they were the *laos*, the people of God; and one of the major differences between then and later was that this word *laos* was used as an *inclusive* term, to describe those counted 'in' as part of the people of God; it is now used as an *exclusive* term, to refer to those who are not as 'in' as the clergy. Formerly the *laos* were the ones with whom God made covenant; now they are the ones who do as they are told. Strictly speaking, ordained priests are still part of the laity, but it is rare for a priest to recognise that privilege. It is time that we stripped away the accretions of our mottled history, and began to live out the simple truth of the Gospel. All of us are privileged to belong to the *laos*. All of us are called to be priests.

The Eucharist is a community act, performed by and for the people of God. To celebrate the Eucharist in isolation makes sense only if it is consciously done as part of a greater whole. In this it might be likened to love, or to sex: it is defined in terms of relationship and, like love or sex, cannot constitute a sacrament in isolation. Rosemary Radford Ruether defines the Eucharist as a community action and makes clear what part the celebrant should play:

> I believe that we should understand absolution and celebration as community powers, which arise wherever two or three gather in the Lord's name, not powers possessed by a sacerdotal caste. It is the community who celebrate the Eucharist together, just as the Eucharist itself represents their transformed life in Christ. It is they who are to absolve one another by a forgiving, loving life style. They are the ones who are to be converted into the 'body of Christ', not a piece of bread. Persons who have been singled out and trained to act as leaders of the liturgical assembly simply represent the community in its relation to God at this point.[3]

It is because of this corporate nature of our life in Christ that so many of us stay with the Church through times of disillusion and despair. I suspect that most caring Christians have endured periods of anger, disappointment or betrayal by the institutional Church; yet the surprising fact remains that many of us do not shake the dust off our feet and cut all links with the Church. Why is this? Why do we doggedly persist in throwing in our lot with an institution that can distress and fail us at least as much as it builds us up and helps us to live christian lives?

One reason is that we understand that following Christ is not being involved in a cosy personal religion, but sharing in the community of all the redeemed. Christianity is not a do-it-yourself religion. What we are doing is seeking the truth, and we are more likely to grasp some of that truth if we have access to different people from all countries and cultures and through all time. We belong to one holy, catholic and apostolic Church.

We should also not underestimate the strength of the Church as a solace and rock for weak human beings. As an individual Christian I may be free to doubt, argue, rage and dismiss the life of faith; or I can struggle on with varying degrees of doubt or confidence. But I know that however lost I may be, I can slip into a church and be carried into prayer and praise, even when that worship is conducted by Christians who are as lost and wayward as I am. For that we can thank God.

There are and have been, no doubt, some Christians who can get along perfectly well without the Church. In some situations people have no choice. But most of us are not strong enough by ourselves, so we lean on the Rock of the Church. But as we do that, it is important that we accept that we *are* the Church, not spectators. What the Church is, is created by people like us, to give strength to each other.

One of the main ways in which Christians through the ages have drawn strength from the Church is through the sacraments, which is why this life blood of the people of God must be safeguarded. As we explore ways in which sacramental grace may be made available to more people and the work of the Church extended in order to bring in the promised reign of God, it is as well to remember the way in which many of the reformed churches have, to greater or lesser extent, been robbed of sacraments.

The sacrament of priesthood is celebrated in our common baptismal priesthood. In the next chapter we must explore what the role of the ordained priesthood is within this.

13

Redefining ordination within the priesthood of all believers

Priesthood is a sacrament, for it reveals to us the nature of God through the ordinary things and people of our lives. It is a sacrament to which we are all called, and part of responding to the Gospel of Jesus Christ is entering, imperfectly and humbly, into that sacrament.

If all are called to partake of this sacrament, the question inevitably arises as to whether we need ordained priests at all. If all are called to priesthood, and all have the duty and the right to perform priestly functions, what is the ordained priesthood for? Most branches of the Christian Church have invested vast financial resources in their ordained clergy, and if it transpired that ordained priests were doing nothing that was not being done equally well by the non-ordained, sweeping economies could be effected by offering their clergy immediate redundancy. If ordination does fulfil a necessary function in the Church, we need to discover how this function differs from that required of the priesthood of all believers. What is the relationship between the baptismal and the ordained priesthood?

The need for ordained priests

From what we have discovered of priesthood in the last chapter, it would appear that priesthood, whether baptismal or ordained, is a desperately difficult business. If our priesthood involves presenting God to the world and the world to God and living self-sacrificial lives, many of us would be only too happy to invent something called the laity that

would absolve us from such expectations. Presenting God
to the world and the world to God brought crucifixion to
one who was far better qualified to do this than we are; and
being called to offer sacrifice is not the sort of vocation most
of us would rate very highly. Even if we want to live out this
sacrificial priesthood, we do not know where to start.

Priesthood is demanding and costly; and if we do try to
exercise our priesthood, we soon become deeply aware of
our failure and inadequacy. This is why we need ordained
priests; not so that some people can cling on to sacred
actions and words, but so that the priesthood of all can be
strengthened, affirmed and developed. If the ordained priest
has any role to play in the Church and in the world, it is to
enable the priesthood of all believers first to realise, and then
to practise their priesthood in the world. This is an
immensely high calling, and one that demands a reassessment of the training and support that the Church offers her
ordained ministry. Such an enabling priesthood is difficult,
challenging, rewarding, holy work; and it is nearer to the
servant model that we find in the gospels than to synods,
consecrations or clerical clubs. It is not about wearing fancy
clothes, or drawing an income from the Church, or saying
words at a service that no one else is allowed to say. It is
about living in a certain way as members of a holy priesthood. It involves making sacraments more available rather
than limiting them. It involves exploring with all those who
have been baptised into priesthood, what it means to be the
guardians of prayer and sacraments.

Even now there are ordained priests who fulfil such functions; who, to the best of their ability within the present
structure, encourage and enable others in their priesthood.
This is remarkable when such qualities play no part in either
the job description or training of clergy. But such priests are
few and far between, and in many cases we are simply
ordaining the wrong people to do the wrong work.

Whom should we be ordaining?

If it is true that the Christian community needs priests to help the whole people of God to recognise and practise their priesthood, then who should be ordained to undertake this important work?

We saw that in the early Church the prophets were those people who regularly prophesied and the teachers those who were found to be good at teaching. In a Church where all are taking their priesthood seriously and trying to live it out, the men and women we should be ordaining as priests are those who clearly have a special aptitude for exercising priesthood. The only people who should be presented as candidates for ordination are those who are already *recognised by the Christian community as priestly*.

In other words, ordination involves the recognition of certain gifts and capacities, not the bestowal of them. So a community may require one of its members to be ordained because he or she celebrates the Eucharist well. Others may have proved themselves to be gifted at motivating and guiding the whole community to create meaningful and beautiful worship and sacraments. One may qualify for ordination because the wounds he has suffered in living life to the full have given birth to a wisdom that teaches others how to live through their own crucifixions and find the God of resurrection within them. Another because her joy and love of God bubbles over into everyone she meets, or because when she preaches or teaches she is able to express truths that others know in their hearts but cannot put into words.

All these qualities can be commonly found within the priesthood of all believers; and it is only because all *can* do these things that it makes sense to ordain some because they do them particularly well. By recognising them and ordaining those who exemplify them, the Christian community is able to make a statement that this is what they mean by Christian priesthood. But the qualities that are being recognised are those that rightfully belong to and are exercised within the priesthood of all believers. That is what priesthood is about.

Such priests would be visible signs of what we mean by our priesthood. They would be signs, not because they are perfect human beings, or perfect priests, for they are unlikely to be either, any more than ordained priests are now. Rather they would make a statement, through their ordinariness, of what Christian priesthood is really about; and affirm the belief of the Church that human beings can live their lives according to the Gospel. They would not become 'professional' priests, for priesthood is necessarily amateur. Even under the present system, very few ordained people would claim that being a priest makes the Christian life any easier for them. They struggle like everyone else; or, if they give up struggling, they fail in their priesthood. Some might imagine that being employed to concentrate on being a priest full time can at least make it easier to pray, or to exercise charity in daily life. Experience, however, suggests that this is not so.

If the Christian community chooses someone to be a priest because of the way in which they are already exercising their priesthood, that person is in a position to *represent* the whole Christian community, by being a statement of what their priesthood is and means. They would not represent all because they were ordained: they would be ordained because they represented what priesthood is and means to all. This function is brought out in the prayer over the new priest in the Book of Common Prayer: 'So that as well by these thy Ministers, as by them over whom they shall be appointed thy Ministers, thy holy Name may be for ever glorified, and thy blessed kingdom enlarged.' We are not absolved from glorifying God or enlarging the kingdom just because someone else has been ordained. But these people are a sign to us and to the whole world, that such things are important.

This does not mean that those we ordain are set apart from other people, though many have misunderstood ordination to imply this. In ordaining someone as a priest we assert that this person represents us all, but is still one of us.

The ordained ministry is representative, not vicarious. It does not stand over against the laity, mediating between

them and God and doing what they cannot. It is commissioned by the head and body alike to do in the name
of the whole what in principle all can do.[1]

To understand ordained priesthood as representative is not
new. R. C. Moberley drew attention to it at the end of the
nineteenth century when he wrote that the ordained priest
is 'the representative and organ of the whole body in the
exercise of prerogatives and powers which belong to the body
as a whole.'[2]

If ordination were to be understood in these terms it would
become a simple act, performed whenever the Christian
community wished to mark the fact that one of their number
is exercising priesthood. It would be a public recognition of
those in whom the Church sees priesthood most clearly
being lived. It might become considerably more common;
and it might be understood as a more temporary state than
the present ordained priesthood is. But there is no reason
why recognition of one's priestly role should bring any more
rights and privileges to that person than to anyone else; and
being priestly, in itself, should carry no remuneration, any
more than being saintly or being efficient does. It is a way
of living, not a job.

St Paul accepts the provisional nature of many priestly
functions in 1 Corinthians 13: 'whether there be prophecies,
they shall fail; whether there be tongues, they shall cease;
whether there be knowledge, it shall vanish away' (v. 8). It
is enough that we should be called to exemplify priesthood
while we have particular gifts to offer. These gifts may
well be temporary, and our ordination should not outlive
them.

If some Christians are ordained because they celebrate
well, they will often, for that same reason, be invited to
celebrate the Eucharist. But this is not something that should
become their right; and their empowerment does not imply
the disempowerment of others. The priest who is recognised
as celebrating well has a duty to teach others how to celebrate
equally well; the eloquent preacher should be training others
to preach; the person who is gifted at creating worship is

needed not just to fulfil this function for as long as they are able, but to enable others to do it so that they themselves can become dispensable. Those in whom the priestly people recognise qualities of priesthood, would therefore be ordained to help others to realise and exercise their own priesthood.

Exercising priesthood through enabling

The greatest disadvantage of the present system of ordination is that it disempowers those who are not ordained, the 'also rans'. Is it possible to develop a vision of ordained ministry as a vocation to enable the priesthood of all believers? Rather than being ordained to limit the sacraments and to cut down the number of priests, ordination should contribute to the growth of the priesthood and make the sacraments more widely available. In other words, the main function of ordained priesthood is *enabling* the priesthood of all believers to recognise and exercise their priesthood in the world. There is no other function or duty that should take precedence over this. There is no other measure of whether someone has exercised an effective priesthood.

If all are called to priesthood, those who are ordained have a duty to help others to hear that call and respond to it. It takes time for people to take on the full responsibility of being members of the priesthood of all believers; only those who have trodden the same path can lead others. In *The Ministry and the Laity*, John Robinson explores what the relationship between ordained and lay Christians should be, and he quotes Hans Rudi Weber: 'The laity are not helpers of the clergy so that the clergy can do their job, but the clergy are helpers of the whole people of God, so that the laity can be the Church.'[3] To be the Church is to be part of the Church's priesthood; it is up to the ordained to help others learn how to live out that priesthood in the world.

In order to be the Church, many people need the strength and inspiration of the sacraments, and part of the work of the priest is to release the potential energy that is in the sacraments into the Church and the world.[4] An enabling priest, rather than striving to fence things in, will open the sacraments to make them available to all who need or would benefit from them. That will mean helping others to create liturgy, and training them to administer the sacraments with sincerity, dignity and understanding.

Sacrament and word

At an ordination service, the prospective priest, in response to questions by the bishop or other senior cleric, makes various promises. At the Anglican ordination, for instance, the candidate promises to accept certain beliefs; to minister doctrine and sacraments; to argue and fight for the true faith where necessary; to maintain diligence in prayer, Bible reading and study; to model themselves and their family on Christian principles; to work for quietness, peace and love in the Christian community; to obey their superiors.

All but one of these requirements are just as applicable to lay people in the Church, and no ordained priest would attempt to prevent a lay Christian from assenting to the same beliefs or striving to live in the same way. The only one of these promises the ordained claim as their sole prerogative, is the second. The whole priesthood of all believers is expected to believe, to argue and fight for the true faith, to pray, study the Bible and live their faith in their personal and family life; but it is only the ordained who can minister doctrine and sacraments. This is where power begins to creep into our understanding of ordination, and to sully the sacraments that should be transparent channels of grace.

The world is in need of sacraments, and part of the Church's role is to make these more available so that as many people as possible may come to know and love God. If the ordained priesthood fences the sacraments in, not only are opportunities for communion with God lost, but the nature of the sacraments themselves is subtly altered. As with the ordinand's other promises, this is a duty that is laid on all who have been baptised into priesthood. Part of our priesthood is, or might on occasions be, to minister the sacraments and word.

However, just because all are called to the priesthood of all believers, this does not mean that all are equally able or willing to preach the word, lead congregations in worship or celebrate the Eucharist. That is why it is appropriate to choose those who are best able to do these things. Those who are chosen to preach are likely to have received a grounding in theological education, those who are to lead worship will probably have developed qualities of leadership, and those who are required to celebrate will have both an understanding of eucharistic theology and a profound and thorough acquaintance with the sacrament.

For Christians for whom the Eucharist is at the core of their worship and life, it is essential that each celebration should be consistent with the tradition of the Church and conducted to the highest standards. The widening of the pool of those who can celebrate should not lead in any way to licence or a diminishing of respect for the sacrament. Good order has always been necessary to maintain the life and worship of the Church; choosing the best, rather than accepting those who have jumped through the various hurdles of theological college and ordination, should help to ensure this.

If an ordained priest is available, it will often make sense for that person to celebrate the Eucharist, since they will, or should, have been ordained because the way in which they do celebrate is pleasing and meaningful to the whole community. But part of the priestly ministry is to make sure that others are also trained, accustomed and enabled to celebrate the Eucharist as necessary. Similarly, ordained priests will often find themselves leading prayer or preaching; but if this is always the case, then they are not fulfilling their prime function as priests.

The priest at the altar

The Eucharist, more than any other single aspect of the Christian religion, exemplifies the two prime functions of priesthood: presenting and sacrificing. At each communion, the celebrant presents the world to God and God to the world, and commemorates and re-enacts the one, perfect and sufficient sacrifice in such a way that it becomes part of the experience of those who share in that sacrament. At the Eucharist, our response of gratitude to God (which is the provenance of the word eucharist) becomes one with our offering of all that we are.

It is right and proper that such an event should be closely associated with priesthood: the priesthood that is shared by all Christians. It is also appropriate that the Church, the royal priesthood, should be able to choose those who consistently present the sacrament in the most meaningful and holy way, to represent them at the altar.

As well as preaching and administering the sacrament, ordained priests bear some responsibility for developing the prayer of the Church. This responsibility often leads to guilt on the part of the ordained, as they recognise that the quality of their own prayer life is no better than anyone else's, and that they are still expected to continue to lead prayer and exhort others to pray when they are passing through dry and stony valleys in their own spiritual life. This imposes unnecessary burdens on the ordained, who should be free to grow in prayer in exactly the same way as everyone else.

The life of prayer is the responsibility of all the royal priesthood, and in this core activity of our lives we cannot hide behind professionals. Most people believe that others enjoy a more fruitful and disciplined prayer life than they do, and that those who are ordained have a hot line to heaven. The reality is that we all fail, and that we need to help each other, as a community of priests, to accept the discipline and the opportunities that prayer offers. The prayers of an ordained priest are no more important or efficacious than the prayers of anyone else. All that one can demand of those who represent us in our priesthood is that they should be *with* people, creating with them their prayer and worship.

There are, however, other tasks that need to be done within the Church, for which it is appropriate to offer remuneration. To separate priesthood from full time Church work would release us to look sensibly at what the Church needs in terms of voluntary and paid workers in order to fulfil its mission in and to the world.

Paid priesthood

Although in St Luke's Gospel we read of Jesus sending the first disciples out to preach the Gospel and instructing them to accept hospitality while engaged in this mission ('for the labourer deserves his wages' Luke 10:7), it was probably more common in the early Church for those in positions of leadership to support the Church than for the community to support them. St Paul himself took pride in the fact that his work as a tent maker (Acts 18:3) enabled him to pay his way, rather than being a drain on the resources of those he was called to serve. 'To this day', he wrote to the Corinthians, '. . . we earn our living by labouring with our own hands' (1 Cor. 4:12).

The Didache, in laying down guidelines for ministry based on what had become general practice in the second century, warns against those who become a drain on Church funds:

> You will be able to distinguish the true from the false. If the newcomer is only passing through, give him all the help you can – though he is not to stay more than a couple of days with you, or three if it is unavoidable. But if he wants to settle down among you, and is a skilled worker, let him find employment and earn his bread. If he knows no trade, use your discretion to make sure that he does not live in idleness simply on the strength of being a Christian. Unless he agrees to this, he is only trying to exploit Christ. You must be on your guard against men of that sort . . . And an apostle at his departure should accept

nothing but as much provisions as will last him to his next night's lodging. If he asks for money, he is not a genuine apostle. (II)

This pattern changed as the Church became a large, powerful and wealthy institution that could not easily be serviced by part-time workers. In Western society there was a long period when the Church offered the only chance of education and civilised employment. Later, those whom the Church engaged knew that, although they were unlikely to amass a great personal fortune, they would be fed, housed, paid and cared for by a wealthy institution for the rest of their lives.

The employment and patronage that the Church has offered, and to some extent is still exercising, is bound to give the institution a large measure of control. There is little doubt that the one who pays the piper calls the tune, and we can see the results of this in such areas as art, where the patronage of the Church meant that for centuries the major works of art that were produced were almost exclusively religious. Universal, established and nonconformist churches alike exercise the ultimate control over their ordained members, as the paying institution ultimately has the right to withdraw financial support to those who wander too far from the current orthodoxy. It should not, therefore, come as any great surprise that genuine prophecy is so rarely associated with priesthood.

However, it is difficult to see why those on whom the Spirit has fallen in such a way as to lead them into ordained priesthood, should be cut off from the rest of the world by falling outside the money economy. If work for the Church precludes or limits other work, then it is quite reasonable that proper remuneration should be given. The point at which, it might be argued, exercising priesthood should diverge from the normal way of the world, is in our recognition that priesthood is a vocation, and that it should not be viewed as another career choice among others.

To be an ordained priest should mean that someone has been chosen by the Christian community to represent them in their priesthood; that their nature or experience qualifies them to perform certain priestly duties for and on behalf of others; and that they have the time, commitment and ability to enable others to grow in priesthood. None of these qualifications or duties takes a person away from their other work and commitments, and not only do they not require payment, but the introduction of monetary remuneration can damage and invalidate them. On the other hand, reliable, professional church work, undertaken by those who are qualified and able to do it and who may have nothing to contribute in terms of priesthood, should be remunerated on a just and sound basis.

Commissioning

The majority of the work load of an ordained priest, at present, has very little to do with priesthood. This is a cause of distress to many who felt they had a vocation to the priesthood, spent several years in training, and then found themselves fulfilling the function of administrator of a small business or master of ceremonies for one day a week. Others are quite happy with their fund raising or organisational role, but know in their heart of hearts that such work does not qualify them for priesthood.

There is a clear need in the Church for leadership and for full-time workers. If church workers were commissioned to undertake the normal tasks that the Church wants doing, they would find themselves undertaking many of the clergy's current roles. The fact that they were not ordained would make no difference to their work, but it would mean that they knew what they were employed to do, and this should lead to an increase in both efficiency and accountability.

Some of the great structures of government and control that the various churches have erected over the years could well be adapted to take over control of employing and directing these workers, and in this much might be learned from the model of the voluntary sector. No organisation will qualify as a registered charity unless it is organised according to certain rules. One such rule is that those who are paid do not, in fact, run the organisation. Paid staff work for, and are answerable to, executive trustees, who receive no remuneration. It is worth noting, in this connection, that seeking a career in the voluntary sector is one way in which Christians can combine their Christian commitment with living in the real world.

If the role of priest could be separated from the many necessary tasks of keeping the Church on the road, those who were truly called to be priests could exercise their priesthood more effectively, while those who worked full time for the institution of the Church could receive proper training and remuneration. Whereas ordination recognises a person's priesthood, commissioning would be more appropriate for appointing people to jobs. The management of churches is necessary and important work, but it has nothing to do with priesthood.

There is no reason why the same person should not both be ordained and commissioned. Many ordained priests under the present system are indeed able to exercise a genuine priestly ministry at the same time as ably administering their churches. A community might well require someone to exercise their priesthood among them by enabling them to grow in priesthood themselves, and at the same time employ them to look after the accounts, or oversee the maintenance of the building, or be responsible for organising the regular services. But the fact that someone was both ordained as a priest and commissioned as a paid employee of the Church would not mislead them into the mistake of thinking that their priesthood differed in kind from that of other people, or gave them power or privilege within the Church.

The ordination service

Once ordination is separated from power or pay, it can be seen as a symbol of the priesthood we all share. As such it can be a distillation of everything that makes priesthood a sacrament, for it would help us to see and understand the priesthood of Jesus Christ. Priesthood is neither magical – making a person into someone or something that they are not – nor pragmatic – encouraging a job-for-life mentality. It is a sacrament, and the service at which we recognise and confirm someone in their priesthood should be a deep and meaningful celebration of what priesthood is all about.

In discussing marriage, we discovered that the sacrament is the common life lived by the two people who love each other, and that the wedding service marks and celebrates their commitment to that sacrament. The wedding service, or solemnisation of matrimony, is a key event within that sacrament, traditionally marking the start of a new life in which the couple lives the sacrament to the full.

It is possible, in the same way, to understand ordination as a public commitment to living a priestly life. Like marriage it recognises something, rather than creates it. Marriage does not make people love each other: ordination does not make them priests. In the marriage ceremony the service marks, rather than creates, the sacrament, which then begins to unfold. Similarly ordination marks and celebrates priesthood. In that it is as important to all involved as a wedding is to the family and community of the bridal couple.

That is as far as the similarities will go, however, for there is a fundamental difference between marriage and ordination. Although marriage is a sacrament of the love of God, and we are all called to live out the love of God in our lives, the relationship that the married couple embarks on is qualitatively different from all other relationships. Ideally it is the closest they will come in this life to understanding the passionate, enduring, faithful love of God; but it must always fall short of the love of God since it expresses and lives out that love exclusively rather than inclusively. To pick out just one aspect of marriage, sexual intercourse within a marital relationship can transport the partners to heights of rapture in which they understand more of the nature of God, it can teach them about the total self-giving of Jesus Christ, and it can fill them with a new spirit that spills over into the rest

of their lives; but such a holy outcome would be impossible
if they claimed sexual licence with all and sundry. Priesthood, on the other hand, is what all baptised Christians
share while ordination can recognise a person's priesthood,
it does not create it. Sacraments are never laws: some achieve
birth in the Holy Spirit without baptism, others enter into
the self-sacrificial love of God without the Eucharist. Ordination is to help the process of priest-making, to ensure that
some do come to priesthood. Its purpose is not to exclude
others.

As life in Christ is summed up in Eucharist, so priesthood
can be summed up in ordination. It is a sign of priesthood,
not the priesthood itself. Only when this has been recognised
and implemented can we begin to explore what it might
mean to live out a Christian priesthood in the world, without
the professional or financial support of membership of a
professional body. Much thought and work needs to be given
to how an ordained priesthood could support, guide and
enable Christians in this work; and how the priests we choose
to represent us can help us to be the Church, a priestly
people living in the world in which God is incarnate. Much
of what absorbs the energies of the Church at present is just
creating religious activity rather than getting on with that.

The work of the Church, which is the people, which is
the royal priesthood, is to practise charity and forgiveness,
to recognise God in human beings and celebrate the Creator
in the creation; it is to offer gratitude and trust to God; to
travel lightly; to be generous in giving, sharing and caring;
and not to run away from life. None of this has much to do
with most church activities or with clergy training. As
always with Christianity, it turns out to be both too simple
and too difficult.

14

The people of God

There is a clear and widely shared perception that all is not well in the Church. This book has explored the hypothesis that one of the reasons for this lies in the present division between clergy and laity, which is putting impossible burdens on the ordained and disabling the laity from exercising their rightful priesthood. A study of the Scriptures and of Church tradition has been found to offer an alternative model, which would spread the responsibility more evenly and release pent up energy so that the whole Church could live more sacramentally.

What has been presented is an understanding of the Church in which ordained priesthood is defined by reference to baptismal priesthood, rather than laity being defined negatively in relation to ordained priesthood. It has been recognised that there is a role for ordained priests in the Church, and that the purpose of such an ordained priesthood within the priesthood of all believers should be understood in terms of helping others to *realise* and *exercise* their priesthood in the world.

There is, however, no avoiding the dilemma that lies at the heart of a book like this. It is one thing to pursue the logic of what is presented in Scripture and upheld by theological analysis, in order to create a consistent doctrine of priesthood. But we live in the real world of long-established structures, of power and privilege, of apathy on the part of many Christians and a fear of responsibility or change. We must consider what is actually possible in such a world.

In view of

1. the historical insupportability and negative impact of the present system of ordination;
2. the reassessment of the priesthood of all believers, in which we have been engaged;
3. the contingency of widespread dissatisfaction with the Church; and
4. advances in biblical scholarship,

how can we address the problem of priesthood radically, without marginalisation? In order to do this it is imperative that any movement comes as a groundswell within the Church, and is not hived off into a reform movement.

How can the vision of Christian priesthood that we have traced be recognised by the different church hierarchies, and become part of the lived experience of all Christians? Is it possible to escape from the long cycle of reform and degeneration that dogs the history of the Christian Church, so that we can start living out the covenant relationship with God that our hearts believe is possible? How can we begin to work towards a future which maintains the Church, does not threaten the clergy, and allows for the growth and development of all Christians? What practical steps can ordained priests take in order to fulfil their vocation of helping others to realise and exercise their priesthood?

It would be unrealistic to expect the pope, the archbishops and patriarchs to capitulate immediately and reorganise the vast edifice of the Church to accommodate the ideas that are here presented; and this, in any case, is not the way in which the Church operates. The Church, with its labyrinthine structures, was not invented or created. It grew; and that growth has always been organic and slow. The Christian community has experimented and rejected, taken blind alleys, made ghastly mistakes and stumbled upon grace and truth. There is no reason to believe that the Church on earth can change and grow in any other way.

We might feel that, in seeking a Church that was true to itself and to the Gospel, we would not start with the present institution. However, we must take the Church as it is, and look initially at what can be done to adapt the existing structures. It is also important to have our eyes open so that we can appreciate the signs of hope that are already stirring in the churches.

Much of the necessary change, in any case, might well come through the action of the Holy Spirit. If the number of people coming forward for ordination does not grow dramatically there will not be enough ordained priests to service the Church, let alone exercise a ministry in the world. Financial constraints, too, mean that not all the clergy who have been ordained can be guaranteed paid employment, and as a result of this, a number of church buildings are at risk of closure. Lay people will have to be prepared to undertake some of the work that has previously been done by ordained priests, and the necessary systems of training and supervision should be put in place with the minimum of delay.

In addition to these pragmatic considerations, there is a change of consciousness in the churches. The experimentation with models of community in the 1960s and 70s and the evolution of housegroups in the 80s and 90s have given many lay people new experiences of being Church, and the relative freedom of such groups is unlikely to be relinquished. All that is necessary is that we now build on what has been achieved.

This book inevitably offers more questions than answers, for its purpose is to initiate discussion. For too long priesthood has been the preserve of the few, and consideration of what priesthood is and means has been left, by and large, to them. If, on the contrary, it transpires that priesthood is something that is shared by all Christians by virtue of their being baptised into the Church, then the discussion can become wider-ranging, and our doctrine of priesthood more exciting and unpredictable.

There really is nothing new in the priesthood of all believers. Not only is it one of the linchpins of the Reformation, but it is quite clearly a concept that carries New Testament validity. It is deep within the Church's understanding of baptism and membership of the Church, and many church documents pay lip service to it. For example, the Anglican Advisory Board of Ministry, in its report on ministry in 1993, states:

> Ordained ministers have a distinctive ministry in the Church but this should not be considered separately from the ministry of the whole people of God who share in the mission and ministry of the Church and of God. The particular ministry of the ordained is to focus, represent and give order to the ministry of the Church and through serving after the pattern of Christ to feed and sustain the people of God for the task of doing God's work in the world.[1]

The point at which vision and practice meet is in the question of how ordained priests can fulfil their role of helping others to realise and exercise their priesthood. What steps can we take, now, to encourage the whole Church to begin to live out its priesthood in the world?

Action

1. Understanding

The first practical outcomes that can be hoped for are that this book will both open up debate about the priesthood of all believers, and also make lay Christians more aware of the responsibility and privilege they share as members of that royal priesthood. Such an understanding of priesthood would go a long way towards building up the Church. Understanding and accepting one's own priesthood is bound, in time, to change the way one lives and works. If we are all members of the priesthood, then we all share responsibility for the work and growth of the Church and have a right to a say in matters of church policy and management. As priests, we have a duty not only to develop our own spiritual life, but also to care about the prayer and worship of the community to which we belong.

As people come to understand that they have a responsibility to live as priests in the world, so their confidence in their own priesthood will grow. They do not have to be surrogate clergy in order to serve the Church: they have to develop their lay priesthood to the full. The Catholic Information Service warns against the dangers of confusing roles:

> It is a reflection on our church when people do not recognise their roles. A lay person who wishes to become active in the church automatically joins an élite . . . However, as more laity become involved in the work of the church, this danger becomes less.[2]

A false doctrine of priesthood has held sway in the Church for far too long. It has robbed baptism of its true meaning, isolated the clergy, disabled the laity and generally been counter-productive for the Church. The mistake is not that the Church practises ordination, but that ordination is tied to a profession within the Church.

Even while the Church does not ordain those whose priesthood is recognised by the rest of the Christian community, Christians can start to value the priestly nature and ministry of those among them who are living out their baptismal priesthood. These people do not need ordination to make them priests, and there is much they can do even within the present system to enable us all in our priesthood.

Priesthood brings with it work and responsibility. We are called to present Christ to the world and the world to Christ; to live sacrificially; and to offer all that we are to God. Our ordinary living should bring blessing to those around us, and we should have the confidence to show others that they are both forgiven and blessed. To accept such responsibilities and to claim such rights will alter the face of the Church even while the structures remain unchanged.

2. Employment

It is likely to be many years before the Church finds ways to enable the exercise of priesthood by all its members. The development of a clearer doctrine of priesthood, however, could release us to take a long, hard and sensible look at what the Church needs in terms of voluntary and paid workers to fulfil its mission in and to the world today. Radical as these ideas may sound, the implementation of them does not demand very much dramatic change. It should be possible, within the existing system, to work towards changing the general consciousness of what priesthood is. Even while theological colleges continue to train for ordained priesthood and the Church to employ and pay clergy, a fresh approach will allow both ordained and lay people to become more aware of their priesthood and to become truly excited and inspired as they develop and offer that in and to the world.

In order to work towards the priesthood of all, it is not necessary that all who are ordained should cease to celebrate the sacraments, nor that all lay people should immediately take on this role. Anyone with extensive experience of leading worship and celebrating the sacraments would be likely to find themselves being used in this way: one might even go so far as to say that it actually makes sense for an ordained priest to celebrate in general, so long as others are trained, accustomed and enabled to do so as necessary. However, it is the responsibility of the whole Church to work towards a future in which there is no necessity for a few ordained Christians to fulfil the priestly functions that all are equally called to exercise.

There are interim measures that could be explored, which would both alleviate the shortage of ordained priests and begin to move the Church's consciousness in the right direction. The hierarchies of the different churches might decide to expand their present understanding of ordained priesthood gradually, by inviting certain people to accept ordination, as was the practice until quite recent times. This would not involve constitutional or theological changes and would, at very little cost, bring about an influx of able and committed workers. For example, the Roman Catholic and Anglican Churches could formally recognise the priesthood of all the superiors of their various orders; the Church of England could ordain readers and the Methodist Church its local preachers. There could be more encouragement of non-stipendiary and worker priests, and some leading theologians, lay leaders and spiritual directors might be persuaded to accept ordination.

In all these cases, the emphasis would be on inviting those who have already demonstrated their suitability, to offer their priestly ministry to the Church. This would immediately make more sense of the concept of obedience to the call of God to be ordained than the present system of personal predilection, theological training and application to boards allows. By leaving them in their own milieu, where they are already exercising their priesthood, rather than appointing them to a church post, this would help to break the expectation that priesthood is about being paid by the Church. It would also tear our concept of Church away from the inward-looking ecclesiastical structures and out into the real world where the majority of God's people live and work, play and suffer, love and die.

3. Ceremony and sacrament

Although there is clearly a need to change our basic assumptions about priesthood, many of the outward forms of the Church might remain practically unchanged. If those who celebrate well, for instance, are invited by the Christian community to represent them at the altar, the majority of Christians will continue to exercise their ministries in other ways than this. Consequently, in reality much the same few people might celebrate the Eucharist regularly as do now. All that would change would be their exclusive right to claim this as their prerogative, and their responsibility for enabling others to perform the same task. They would continue to explore what it means to consecrate the bread and wine, continue to find ways in which they might make this sacrament more meaningful and holy for the community. They would still be ordained as priests, say the same words and could wear the same vestments.

If part of the duty of the priest, however, is to enable others to exercise their priesthood, there will be times when those who are not ordained will, in particular circumstances, be called upon to celebrate. Any baptised Christian would have the right, and should be trained to develop the ability, to celebrate all the sacraments of the Christian Church, including the Eucharist.

Many Christians will wish to wait until the rules change before they accept the sacraments from those who have not been officially ordained; and those who do not feel so constrained should respect the patience and self-denying waiting of such people. Others will follow the logic that is suggested by a study of the priesthood of all believers, and in a spirit of holy disobedience, find themselves led to break the present rules. Within both camps there is ample room for experimenting with creating forms of service and community liturgy, and for exploring the nature and power of the sacraments.

In the same way that reformers need to retain the sacraments at the centre of their worship, rather than being excluded from them by the institutional Church and hived off into reform movements, so it is important to maintain the dignity, richness and beauty of the sacraments while daring to depart from some of their traditional aspects. Those who are moved by music, or vestments, or incense, or icon, or whatever else should maintain those elements, even if they also explore new ones such as choreography, stones or candle light. Special garments have a place in many of the sacraments, and in some parts of the world the whole congregation puts on special clothes for the Eucharist.

Some people in the Church would no doubt feel threatened by the issues raised in this book, and those who are led to pursue the logic may well find their efforts receive scant thanks or appreciation. There is, however, still a place in the world and in the Church, for prophets who are prepared to dare great things for what they believe is right. And all Christians have the right to be rooted and grounded in the sacraments that are their life-blood.

4. Training and theology

Talk of the priesthood of all believers can raise anxieties for lay Christians who feel they are not qualified to fulfil the functions of priests. Such anxieties are groundless, since the whole point of priesthood being recognised by the

Christian community is that one would only be invited to do things that one was able to do.

The corollary of this, however, is that training should be available to all Christians so that the necessary qualities and talents can be fostered and developed. Such training should not aim to produce professional Christians or imitation clergy; nor should it encourage anyone to adopt a position in the Church that differentiates them from others. Rather it should seek to raise the theological level of the whole Christian community and ensure that all Christians are learning how to live out their priesthood in the world.

> What we need is not more special training sessions to persuade laity that they have a role in the Church. That ought to be self-evident; and most committed lay people sit through at least one full-length sermon each week, which should be training them for ministry in the world.[3]

While this is true, it must also be admitted that the sermons many Christians are constrained to listen to leave much to be desired in terms of training for the demands of lay priesthood.

The other important feature of training is that it can play an important part in maintaining the consistency and unity of the Church, by controlling some of the worst excesses of a theological free for all. One of the difficulties of the changes advocated in this book is the question of how we can maintain a common *theology* that allows progress and development of thought within a consistent and universally accepted framework? How can the unity of the Church be maintained?

Such a consistent theology, of course, is not safeguarded by the present system, as is evident in the myriad shades of meaning and understanding adopted by different denominations, or the furore that attends some of the utterances of academic theologians. However, most of the differences between denominations do not stem from theological differences, but from tradition and practice; and the best theologians from different denominations generally find more to agree than disagree about. Catholicity of belief is more likely to come from open and intelligent study of theology than from blindly obeying the edicts of clergy who are concerned to maintain their denominational boundaries. In this way, ecumenism stands to gain from a heightened appreciation of the priesthood of all believers.

As theological education is moved higher up the agenda for all Christians, more people will be qualified to make informed judgements about the utterances of theologians, and to explore their faith in the more intellectual and ecumenical spirit that theological study can foster.

One of the joys of working, as I do, for Feed the Minds[4] is that I am frequently required to visit some of the lay education programmes that have developed in the two-thirds world in response to the rapid growth of Christianity. Through these 'theological education by extension' programmes, Christians from all walks of life are able to receive a thorough grounding in theology without leaving their homes or normal employment. Whatever happens to the institution and hierarchy of the Church in some of the difficult situations faced by the young churches in the developing world over the coming years, the Gospel will be proclaimed, and the people nurtured and led, by committed lay people who have been well trained to exercise their leadership and ministry.

5. Claiming baptismal unity

Many will be unsure about their ability or desire to exercise priesthood in any very obvious way. However, apart from their membership of the priesthood of all believers, there is another, even more basic right, that has been denied to many millions of baptised Christians.

Baptism is into the Christian Church, not into a particular denomination; and all baptised Christians have the right to claim membership, and receive the sacraments of, the various parts of the universal Church. The Daily Missal of the Roman Catholic Church defines one of the effects of baptism to be that it 'gives us the right to take part in divine worship, i.e. in Holy Mass, Holy Communion'.[5] Yet most denominations either do, or have in the past sought to, maintain their identity by refusing to share their sacraments with any who have not taken out official membership of that denomination. This is particularly true of the sacrament of holy communion, or Eucharist, so central to the mainstream denominations. This sacrament of unity, far from reflecting our oneness in Christ or our common celebration of reconciliation, has itself become a symbol of disunity.

By recognising baptism as our initiation into the priesthood of all believers, we are in a position to insist on our essential unity. While the ordained priesthood may be concerned to control and sharpen distinctions between the various denominations, the priesthood of all believers has the right to live as one Church, one body of Christ. Rather than being subject to history, and trying to squeeze ourselves into one or other of the divided churches, we are offered the liberty to live as post-denominational Christians.

The fate of the Anglican/Methodist debate on church unity at the end of the 1960s is a warning of the way in which the power of the ordained clergy can work through ecclesiastical structures and run counter to the wishes of the Church. The scheme was accepted by the Methodist Conference and by the Houses of Laity and Bishops at the General Synod of the Church of England. Like the first vote on the ordination of women in the Anglican Church, however, it was defeated in the House of Clergy. The two churches therefore went their separate ways; but the way in which shared ministry has developed and relationships flourished between the lay people of these denominations since that time offers real hope that ecumenism, as opposed to church unity, can grow from the grass roots.

By turning away from the stranglehold of ordination, all Christians are given another chance to override denominational differences by attempting to remain in communion with the whole Church. Freedom to disregard the evils of church division is one of the distinguishing features of lay Christianity. It is sincerely to be hoped, and expected, that a reassessment of priesthood will bring this liberty to the whole Church, so that ecumenism can be breathed freshly and vigorously into even the topmost corners and crannies of the ecclesiastical structures.

The priesthood of all believers, by rejoicing in being lay, is in a position to remain in communion with the whole Church – whatever that might be. Different rules apply in the different denominations; but there is room within them all for people to be creative in exploring and challenging the different rules and systems. There is no reason why Christians should not struggle towards a more biblical and sacramental understanding of priesthood within their own contexts: finding ways in which to work creatively in order to remain true to their various traditions.

As lay people come to realise that they themselves are, indeed, the Church, and that they have the right and responsibility to live in such a way as to bring in the promised reign of God, they are less likely to be deflected from their mission of reconciliation by submitting to the present structures. What the Church now is, has come to us from history: what it will become in the future is in our hands.

6. Being the Church and exercising priesthood

The most important practical step that can be taken towards this new vision of priesthood, is for lay and ordained Christians to work within the Church to help a new consciousness come to birth and grow. It is imperative that any movement for change comes as a groundswell within the Church, and is not hived off into a reform movement. To ache and cry for the Church is a call to become more involved, not to abandon ship. It is a truism that institutions are more effectively changed from within than without, and this means that those who are working and praying for change need to be prepared to persevere and militate in the Church, at the risk of unpopularity and rejection.

Those who have not been ordained need to be encouraged to rejoice in their status as lay people, members of the priesthood of all believers, and not to interpret that as an excuse for learned helplessness. They are fortunate in being able to live out their Christian priesthood in the world. On the other hand they may need to be encouraged to claim their priesthood and to accept responsibility for exercising their ministry. Clearly, lay people who are fully involved in living and working in the world will be too busy to run the Church as well. But perhaps it is time that they saw those who are employed by the Church as their employees, who are commissioned to work with and for them.

If the laity would *own* the Church and could demand accountability from those employed in its service, there might be much more willingness to tithe both time and money for the work of the Church. Several branches of the Church wonder why church giving does not rise more. Many lay people would answer this by saying they are not confident that money they give to the church collection is well used. Propping up ancient monuments or cutting clergy lawns are not generally considered high priorities for Christians who are more concerned about the poverty and injustice in the world and would rather give their money to charities that address such suffering directly. If lay people had a real say in how the Church's assets were used, there would be much more motivation to give, and a system of tithing might well become a normal part of Christian life.

In a Church which recognised the priestly nature of its people, there would also be a case for the tithing of time. Most Christians want to contribute to the Church, but as the work load of those who are still in employment increases, there is less commitment to engaging in church activity for the sake of it. If, on the other hand, lay people know that they are needed to help someone, or to lead a meeting, or plan worship, or balance the church accounts, or visit the sick, these activities will receive higher priority.

But above all, members of the royal priesthood should be enabling and supporting each other. Lay people enjoy greater freedom than those who are employed by the Church, and there are many ways in which they can begin to live out their priesthood and become true bearers of sacramental grace even within the present system. It is our responsibility and should be our delight to celebrate life in Christ and to live sacramentally. This does not just apply to the sacraments of the Church that we examined in chapters 9 to 11, but to the whole of life which should bear the imprint of the divine and reveal God to us.

For example, there are countless opportunities for blessing people, both sacramentally and casually. Every day life is full of potential for incarnating God, for invoking the Holy Spirit, for initiating prayer and sacrament. Through discovering these opportunities and humbly doing the work that is given them to do, lay people will gain more confidence in exercising their own priesthood. They enjoy greater freedom, simply by being lay; and they should be encouraged to rejoice in that freedom and exercise it to the full. They have priceless opportunities for breaking through denominational rules, for growing into communion with the whole Church, even for creating worship and liturgy that are accessible to people who do not fit comfortably into the established institutions. The priesthood of all believers stretches across all the churches, and those in the different denominations will find varying ways in which to exercise their ministries. Above all, by identifying with the priesthood of Christ, we commit ourselves to living lives of reconciliation, both within the Church and in the wider world.

The Church does not need more ordained clergy. It needs more people who are aware that they are called to be a royal priesthood. All are called, but if our vocation is to the laity, our baptism still makes us priests.

> You are a chosen race, a kingdom of priests, a holy nation, a people to be a personal possession to sing the praises of God who called you out of the darkness into his wonderful light. (1 Pet. 2:9)

Notes

Chapter 1: On being the Church

1 That council addressed itself to the issue of the lay apostolate in *Apostolicam Actuositatem*, as well as including the priesthood of the faithful in a more general discussion of the Church in *Lumen Gentium*.

2 *Lumen Gentium* 10

Chapter 2: Chosenness and covenant

1 Tony Harrison, v. from Selected Poems, p. 248.

2 See my discussion of the Holy Spirit in terms of *ruah* in chapter 7, *Life-Giving Spirit*.

Chapter 3: Priests and prophets

1 Michael Jenkins, in *Clarion* vol. II, no 5, differentiates prophets from seers: 'The Seers answered questions they were asked, the Prophets answered questions they were not asked.' 'The Relationship Between Bishops and Theologians.'

2 Manuscript note in a Bible of 1875.

3 Edward Schillebeeckx, *Ministry: A case for change* (London, SCM Press, 1981), p. 16.

Chapter 5: Leadership in the early Church

1 Michael Ramsey, *The Christian Priest Today* (London, SPCK 1969), p. 106.

2 James G. D. Dunn, *Unity and Diversity in the New Testament* (London, SCM Press, 1977), ch. VI.
3 Hans Küng, *The Church* (English translation: Search Press, Tunbridge Wells, England, 1968/81), p. 433.
4 Richard Hanson, *The Christian Priesthood Examined* (Lutterworth Press, 1979), p. 27.
5 Edward Schillebeeckx, *Ministry: A case for change* (ET London, SCM Press, 1981), p. 41.
6 Schillebeeckx, p. 41.
7 Kenneth Stevenson, *First Rites* (Lamp Press, 1989), chapter 3.
8 Küng, p. 125.
9 John Robinson, *The Ministry and the Laity*; in *Layman's Church*.
10 Leonard Doohan, *Lay People and the Church*; The Way, vol. 32, no. 3, July 1992, p. 169.

Chapter 6: New Testament theology

1 The inclusion of the Letter to the Hebrews within the canon of Scripture was long challenged and the identity of the writer still elicits a number of interesting theories but no conclusive evidence: Barnabas, Apollos, Aquila and Priscilla.
2 Küng, *The Church*, p. 374.

Chapter 7: History and Reformation

1 Justin, *Dialogue with Trypho* 116.3; Irenaeus, *Adversus Haereses* 4.17; Clement of Alexandria, *Stromateis* 7.7.36.
2 Tertullian, *De Exhortatione Castitatis* 7
3 Tertullian, *De Exhort. Cast.* 7.3.
4 Tertullian, *De Fuga in Persecutione* 14.1.
5 Cyprian of Carthage, *Letters* 63: *PL* 4, 386.
6 Jerome, *Dialogus contra Luciferianos* ch. 21: *PL* 23, 175.
7 The last ban on absolute ordinations was by Pope Innocent in 1189.
8 Guerricus of Igny, *Sermo* 5: *PL* 185, 57.
9 Hippolytus, *Refutatio omnium haeresium* 8.19.
10 Hildegard of Bingen, *Liber divinorum operum* 10.16.
11 Luther, 'The Freedom of the Christian', *Three Treatises* (Philadelphia, Fortress Press, 1966), p. 275.
12 Luther, 'To the Christian Nobility of the German Nation', *Three Treatises* p. 14.

Chapter 8: The impact of ordination on the Church now

1 Leonard Doohan, *ibid*, p. 174.
2 Maggie Ross, *Pillars of Flame: Priesthood and Spiritual Maturity* (SCM Press, 1988), p. 35.
3 A. A. K. Graham, 'Should the Ordained Ministry now Disappear?' in *Theology LXXI*, no 576 (June 1968), p. 244.
4 Jean Tillard, *Church of Churches*; The Liturgical Press, 1992. First published as *Église d'Églises*; Les Editions du Cerf, 1987, ch. 3.
5 *Apostolicam Actuositatem*, 24.
6 *Lumen Gentium* 10, ch. 2.
7 *Apostolicam Actuositatem*, 29.
8 Yves Congar, *Lay People in the Church* (London, Bloomsbury, 1957), p. 24.
9 ibid. p. 455.
10 Michael Ramsey, *The Christian Priest Today* (London, SPCK, 1969), p. 14

Chapter 9: Sacraments

1 Book of Common Prayer Catechism.
2 Peter Lombard, *Sentences* Book 4, dist. i, no 2.
3 Article XXV of the Thirty-nine Articles.
4 Alwyn Marriage, *Life-Giving Spirit: Responding to the Feminine in God* (London, SPCK, 1989), pp. 116–118.
5 The Anglican clergy are, by virtue of being ordained within the established Church, authorised to officiate at weddings in any Church of England church. Clergy of other denominations can be licensed, as individuals, to officiate at weddings within their own church.
6 The situation is, in fact, rather more complicated in the Orthodox Church, where a married man may be ordained, but only the monastic, and therefore celibate, can become bishops.
7 This interpretation of ordination or the religious life is less common now than it used to be.
8 This does not assume any particular level of intelligence; and it is not affected by mental retardation, since such a disability is part of what a person is, and all ways of being human are of equal worth in the eyes of God.
9 Roman Missal: 'The Effects of Baptism' 3.
10 The service of 'churching' can go some way towards answering these needs, though there is scope for improvement and development of such services. In former times, the service of church-

ing was flawed by an underlying negative attitude to women's sexuality and reproduction; but such attitudes have now, in the main, been expurgated. Childbirth is not, and should never be viewed as, something from which we need to be cleansed.

11 Book of Common Prayer, 'General Rubricks of the Ministration of Publick Baptism of Infants'.
12 Daily Missal
13 Alternative Service Book, p. 280.
14 Constitution on the Liturgy, 73.
15 New Rite for Anointing (1974)
16 Francis MacNutt, *Healing* (Ave Maria Press, 1974), pp. 280ff.
17 ibid. p. 249.

Chapter 10: Eucharist

1 See, however, *Quaker Faith and Practice* 27.42: 'This is a testimony which seems to be dying of neglect. Many Friends, involved with family and the wider society, keep Christmas; in some meetings, Easter and its meaning is neglected, not only at the calendar time but throughout the year.'
2 ibid.
3 Gregory Dix, *The Shape of the Liturgy* (Dacre Press, 1945; New York, Seabury Press, 1982), p. 744.
4 Dante, *Paradiso*, Canto XXXIII, line 145.
5 This point was admirably made by Bishop John Austin Baker at a talk for ordinands on lay celebration, at Salisbury and Wells Theological College on February 20 1988.

Chapter 11: Ordination

1 Peter Fink, 'Priesthood' in Alan Richardson and John Bowden, *A New Dictionary of Christian Theology* (London, SCM Press, 1983), p. 466.

Chapter 12: The nature of priesthood for all Christians

1 T. F. Torrance, 'Royal Priesthood', *Scottish Journal of Theology*, Occasional Papers no 3 (Edinburgh, Oliver and Boyd, 1955), p. 87.

2 Douglas Rhymes, 'The place of the laity in the parish', in John Robinson, *Layman's Church* (Lutterworth Press, 1963), p. 33.
3 Rosemary Radford Ruether, 'The Ministry of the People and the Future Shape of the Church' in Catholic Renewal Movement, *People, Power and Priesthood* (Catholic Renewal Movement, 1987), p. 7.

Chapter 13: Redefining ordination within the priesthood of all believers

1 John Robinson, *Christian Priesthood Symposium* (London, Darton, Longman & Todd, 1970), p. 15. See also his *The Christian Priesthood* (London, Darton, Longman & Todd, 1970).
2 R. C. Moberly, *Ministerial Priesthood* (London, John Murray, 1899), p. 258.
3 John Robinson, 'Ministry and the Laity' in *Layman's Church* p. 17.
4 This, clearly, is not the case with Friends and the Salvation Army.

Chapter 14: The people of God

1 Advisory Board of Ministry, 'Ministry in the Church of England' in *The Report of a Working Party on Criteria for Selection for Ministry in the Church of England*, 10.7, p. 52.
2 Catholic Information Service, *Briefing* vol. 9, no 28 (1979), p. 1.
3 Chris Peck, 'The Elusive Laity', letter in *Theology*, January 1984, p. 46.
4 Feed the Minds works on behalf of all the British and Irish churches and missionary societies to fund literacy, literature and communications projects throughout the developing world.
5 See the Daily Missal, 'The Effects of Baptism', p. 1767. Saint Andrew Daily Missal, Biblica, Bruges, Belgium 1958, 1962.

Bibliography

Advisory Board of Ministry, *Report of a Working Party on Criteria for Selection for Ministry in the Church of England.* Policy Paper No. 3A, (1993).

Beasly-Murray, Paul (ed.), *Anyone for Ordination?*, Tunbridge Wells, Monarch Publications, 1993.

Bennet, David W., *Biblical Images for Leaders and Followers*, Regnum Lynx, 1993.

Bettenson, Henry (ed.), *Documents of the Christian Church*, Oxford, Oxford University Press, 1943.

Broadman Bible Commentary, vol. 12, Nashville, Tenn., Broadman Press, 1972.

Catholic Renewal Movement, *Weekday People: Exploring the place of Christian believers in the world today*, 1987.

Chadwick, Henry, 'Lima, ARCIC and the Church of England', *Theology*, LXXXVII no. 715 (January 1984).

Chadwick, Owen, *The Reformation*, Harmondsworth, Penguin Books, 1964.

Coate, Mary Anne, *Clergy Stress: the hidden conflicts of ministry*, London, SPCK, 1989.

Congar, Yves, *Lay People in the Church*, London, Bloomsbury, 1957.

Dante, *The Selected Works* ed. by Paolo Milano, Chatto & Windus, 1972.

Dix, Gregory, *The Shape of the Liturgy*, London, Dacre Press, 1945; New York, Seabury Press, 1982.

Doohan, Leonard, 'Spirituality and Lay Ministry', *The Way*, vol. 32, no. 32 (July 1992), ed. D. Langdale and P. Sheldrake 53.

Dunn, James D. G. *Unity and Diversity in the New Testament*, London, SCM Press, 1977.

Elliot-Binns, Michael, *The Layman and the Church*, Church Information Office, 1970.

Flannery, Austin, OP (ed.), *Vatican Council II: the Conciliar and Post Conciliar Documents*, Costello, 1975.

214   BIBLIOGRAPHY

General Synod Board of Education, *All Are Called – Towards a theology of the laity*, Church Information Office, 1985.
Graham, A. A. L. 'Should the Ordained Ministry now Disappear?', *Theology* LXXI, no. 576 (June 1968).
Hanson, Richard, *Christian Priesthood Examined*, Guildford and London, Lutterworth Press, 1979.
Harrison, Tony, *Selected Poems*, London, Penguin Books, 1984.
Hermann, Siegfried, *A History of Israel in Old Testament Times*, London, SCM Press, 1975.
Hoffman, Virginia, *Birthing a Living Church*, New York, Crossroad, 1988.
Israel, Martin, *Healing as Sacrament*, London, Darton, Longman & Todd, 1984.
Jenkins, Michael, 'The Relationship between Bishops and Theologians ', *Clarion*, vol. II, no. 5.
Kraemer, Hendrick, *A Theology of the Laity*, Guildford and London, Lutterworth Press, 1958.
Küng, Hans, *The Church*, Search Press, 1968/1981.
Luther, Martin, *Three Treatises*, from the American edn of Luther's Works, Philadelphia, Fortress Press, 1966.
MacNutt, Francis, OP, *Healing*, Ave Maria Press, 1974.
Maddocks, Morris, *The Christian Healing Ministry*, London, SPCK, 1981.
Main, John, OSB, *The Christian Mysteries: Prayer and Sacrament*, Benedictine Community of Montreal, 1979.
Marriage, Alwyn, *Life-Giving Spirit: Responding to the Feminine in God*, London, SPCK, 1989.
Moberley, R. C., *Ministerial Priesthood*, London, John Murray, 1899.
Moltmann, Jürgen, *The Spirit of Life: A universal affirmation*, London, SCM Press, 1992.
Murphy, James H. (ed.) *New Beginnings in Ministry*, Columba Press, 1992.
Peck, Chris, 'Elusive Laity', Letters to the Editor, *Theology* LXXXVII no. 715 (January 1984).
Plato, *Protagoras and Meno*, Harmondsworth, Penguin Classics, 1956.
Quaker Faith and Practice, Warwick Printing Company, 1995.
Ramsey, Michael, *The Christian Priest Today*, London, SPCK, 1969.
Ranken, Michael, 'A Theology of the Priest at Work', *Theology* LXXXV, no. 704 (March 1982).
Richardson, Alan, and Bowden, John (eds.), *A New Dictionary of Christian Theology*, London, SCM Press, 1983.
Robinson, John, *On Being the Church in the World*, London, SCM Press, 1960.

Robinson, John, *Layman's Church*, Lutterworth Press, 1963.

Ross, Maggie, *Pillars of Flame: Power, Priesthood and Spiritual Maturity*, London, SCM Press, 1988.

Saunders, E. P., *The Historical Figure of Jesus*, London, Allen Lane, The Penguin Press, England, 1993.

Schillebeeckx, Edward, *Ministry: A case for change*, ET John Bowden, London, SCM Press, 1981.

Smethurst, David, *Extended Communion: An experiment in Cumbria*, St Albans, Grove Books, 1986.

Smethurst, David, *Shared Ministry in the Church of England* M. Phil. thesis, University of Manchester, 1984.

Staniforth, Maxwell (trans.), *Early Christian Writings: The Apostolic Fathers*, Harmondsworth, Penguin Classics, 1968.

Stevenson, Kenneth, *First Rites*, London, Lamp Press, Marshall Pickering 1989.

Tillard, J.-M. R., *Church of Churches*, The Liturgical Press, 1992. First published as *Église d'Églises*, Les Editions du Cerf, 1987.

Torrance, T. F. 'Royal Priesthood', *Scottish Journal of Theology*, Occasional Paper no. 3, Edinburgh and London, Oliver and Boyd, 1955.

Vidler, Alec, 'Religion and the National Church' in Vidler (ed.) *Soundings*, Cambridge, Cambridge University Press, 1962.

The Way, Supplement 47 'Spirituality and Priesthood'.